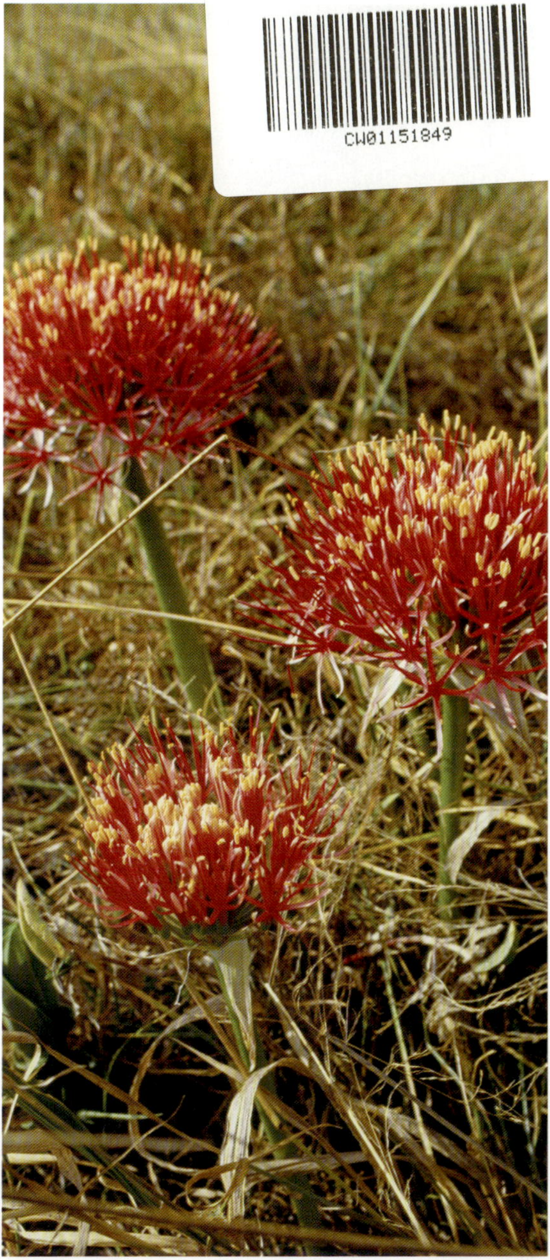

The Beauty of the
Maasai Mara

CAMERAPIX
PUBLISHERS INTERNATIONAL

This book was designed and produced by
Camerapix Publishers International
PO Box 45048, 00100 GPO
Nairobi, Kenya

© David Round-Turner and Camerapix 2007

Revised edition 2007

ISBN: 1-904722-12-1

Production Director: Rukhsana Haq
Editors: Roger Barnard and Jan Hemsing
Design Consultant: Calvin Mackenzie
Creative Team: Sam Kimani, Martin Serem,
    Shakira Ahmed & Rachel Musyimi

All rights reserved. No part of this publication may
be reproduced, stored in a retrieval system, or
transmitted in any means, electronic, mechanical,
photocopying recording or otherwise without permission
in writing from Camerapix Publishers International.

Printed in Singapore.

Front cover: Lion cub growls warning to encroaching photographer.

Back cover: Hot air balloons glide silently over a herd of Thomson's gazelle grazing on the Maasai Mara's lush grasslands.

Half-title: Wild flowers of the savannah.

Title-page: Waterbuck at sundown on the Maasai Mara.

Contents

	Introduction	**9**
1.	The empty Land	**14**
2.	The making of a Game Reserve	**26**
3.	The Maasai People	**32**
4.	The Mara Country	**42**
5.	The grazers and the browsers	**60**
6.	The big shots – Elephant, Buffalo, Rhino	**74**
7.	The Hunters – the Big Cats	**90**
8.	The Hunters – the Lesser Breeds	**108**
9.	Those who also have their being	**118**
10.	Images	**126**

The Mara River wends its way through the Maasai Mara plains to Lake Victoria.

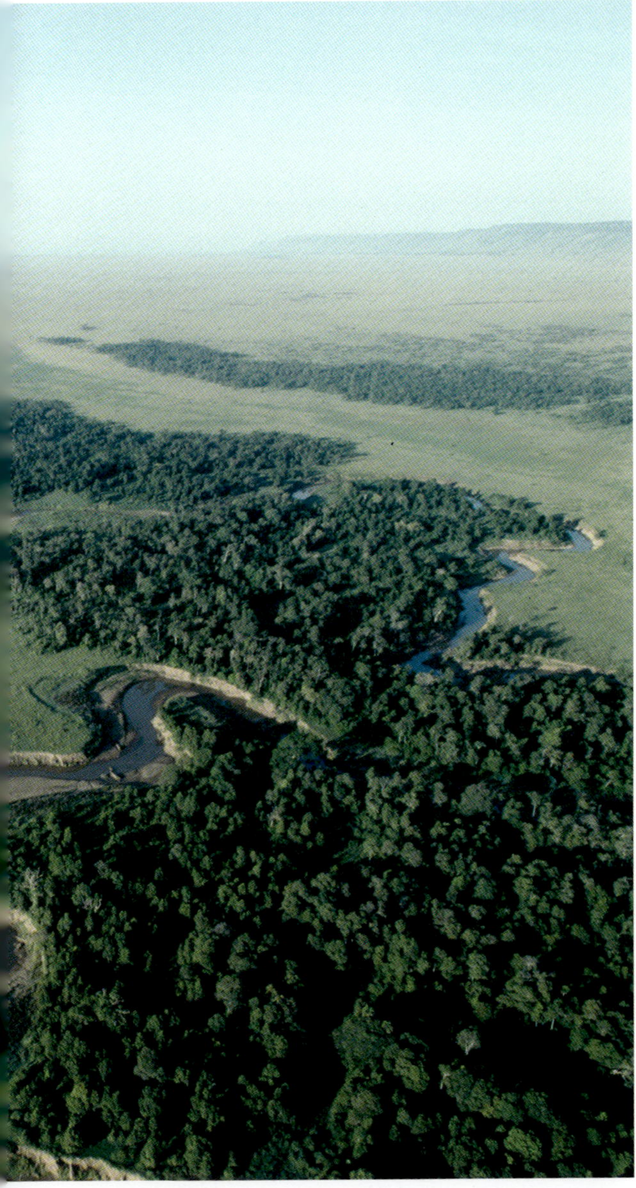

Cheetah cub.

Introduction

Hundreds of thousands of people from all over the world visit Kenya's Maasai Mara National Reserve every year. The magic of the Mara has been articulated in countless books, and captured on film and canvas. Her importance in Africa's complex wildlife mosaic, and the problems that concern her survival, have been the themes of many television documentaries, conservation seminars and papers. Over the years the Mara has acted as a base for scores of wildlife researchers.

Despite all this close attention the Maasai Mara is one of the few places left on earth where wildlife still flourishes, comparatively undisturbed, in the numbers that once roamed the plains and forests of Africa. There may have been a time when the Mara was empty of wildlife, but that would have been unimaginably long ago, well beyond our perception and recent ecological history.

For most of us, wildlife, large and small, has roamed the Maasai Mara from time immemorial. It is difficult to imagine otherwise. Present generations should be grateful that they can experience the magnificence of the Mara, and that modern technology can carry them great distances in comfort and let them live amid the splendour of one of Africa's finest wildlife sanctuaries – that too in the kind of comfort that would not disgrace the world's best hotels.

As the northern tip of the vast Serengeti ecosystem, the Mara hosts the spectacular seasonal migration of many thousands of wildebeest, zebra and attendant predators. It is the dry season refuge for the migrants, and for the large numbers of resident animals. Well-watered, seldom without an ample food supply, whether for the grazers or the hunters, the Mara is unique in containing such a diverse, year-round wildlife population. The impact on the visitor, even the cynical city dweller, can be profound, and few remain unmoved by its magnificence.

Introduction

The Maasai Mara is attractive country, where rounded hills, riverine forest and acacia woodlands break up the monotony of the more dominant grass plains. Rocky outcrops, remnants of the violent volcanic activity that shaped much of Africa, harbour small creatures and, seasonally, wild flowers.

Through it all flows the Mara River. Rising in the highland forests to the north and west of the game reserve, the river winds its majestic way, at times almost looping back on itself as if loath to leave the land to which it lends its name. But the Mara River can be moody. The slow-flowing waters, usually turgid and laden with silt carried from the cultivated lands upstream, can become a raging torrent of destruction after heavy rains have swelled the feeder tributaries. Trunks and branches of full-grown trees, the carcasses of unfortunate animals – people too, sometimes – are swept with immense force amid the thunder of the tumbling waters to be wedged under and against the few bridges, causing logjams, burst banks and floods.

As the rains fall so the colours of the Mara change. The stands of sere grass on the plains turn green and are cropped close by the grazers seeking out their new shoots. Trees, their leaves half shed and the rest wilted, put out new growth – the browns and yellows replaced by a deep green.

The acacias will flower, their early blooms a signal that rain is near. Wild flowers open and blossom, the so-called tissue-paper flower (*Cycnium tubulosum*) litters the ground with its white petals, while the small orange flowers of *Crossandra subacaulis*, the yellow ones of *Crassocephalum* and the dark purple ones of the erect *Hibiscus cannabinus*, give pleasure to the human eye and food for many wild mouths and beaks.

The Maasai Mara lies in southwest Kenya, in the Narok district of Kenya's Maasailand. Most of it is between 1,500 and 1,800 metres above sea level. With an average annual

Introduction

rainfall of some 1,000 millimetres there is usually enough food and water to see the wildlife through the dry months. Averages, however, are misleading, and parts of the area, Musiara to the west and along the river for example, can expect up to 1,500 millimetres a year while the drier south-eastern corner might be lucky to get more than 750 millimetres in some years. The droughts of 1961 and 2006 were unusually severe with many wild animals, especially buffalo, succumbing to starvation.

Even up to the mid-fifties, the Mara was a comparatively little known part of Kenya. It was visited only by safari hunters and the more adventurous administrators, and contained few permanent residents – though the nomadic Maasai grazed sheep and goats in what is now the game reserve. It was popular with the few serious naturalists who knew of it, and occasionally local honey seekers and hunters passed through it.

Today, of course, it has a worldwide reputation and is visited by up to a quarter of a million people each year. An abundance of lodges and camps exist to accommodate these visitors, though few spend more than a day or two – too short a time, alas, to absorb more than a fraction of the Mara's joys and beauty.

From 1961, when the game reserve came into being, the Mara flourished and has delivered up many of its secrets. It has been poetically referred to as pristine Africa, Africa as it always was, unspoiled Africa and similar wishful phrases.

The fact is that Africa is no different from elsewhere. There is constant change, natural as well as that wrought by human endeavour. The Mara, too, has evolved as man and nature have taken their toll. The Mara today is very different from what existed 60 years ago. What existed then is very different from what might have been seen a hundred years ago. Ecologists believe that today's Maasai Mara and its vegetation more closely resemble the land as it was in the latter part of the last century.

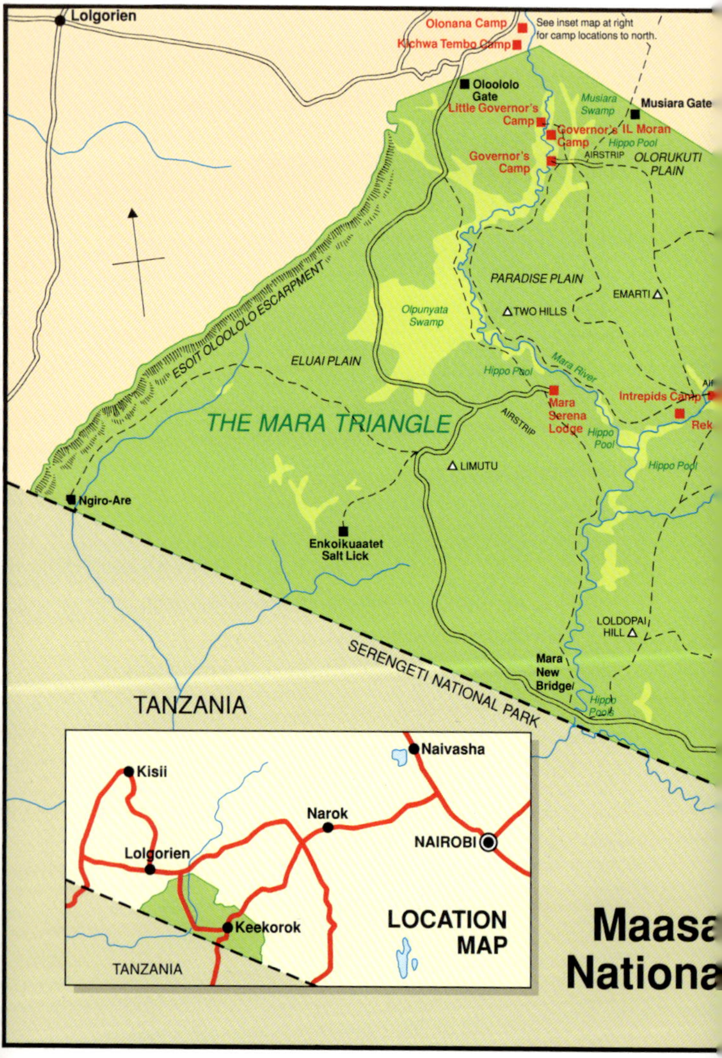

Lolgorien
Olonana Camp
Kichwa Tembo Camp
See inset map at right for camp locations to north.
Oloololo Gate
Musiara Swamp
Musiara Gate
Little Governor's Camp
Governor's IL Moran Camp
Hippo Pool
Governor's Camp
AIRSTRIP
OLORUKUTI PLAIN
ESOIT OLOOLOLO ESCARPMENT
PARADISE PLAIN
EMARTI
TWO HILLS
Olpunyata Swamp
ELUAI PLAIN
Mara River
Hippo Pool
Mara Serena Lodge
Intrepids Camp
AIRSTRIP
THE MARA TRIANGLE
Hippo Pool
Hippo Pool
LIMUTU
Ngiro-Are
Enkoikuaatet Salt Lick
LOLDOPAI HILL
Mara New Bridge
Hippo Pools
SERENGETI NATIONAL PARK
TANZANIA
Naivasha
Kisii
Narok
NAIROBI
Lolgorien
Keekorok
LOCATION MAP
TANZANIA
Maasa
Nationa

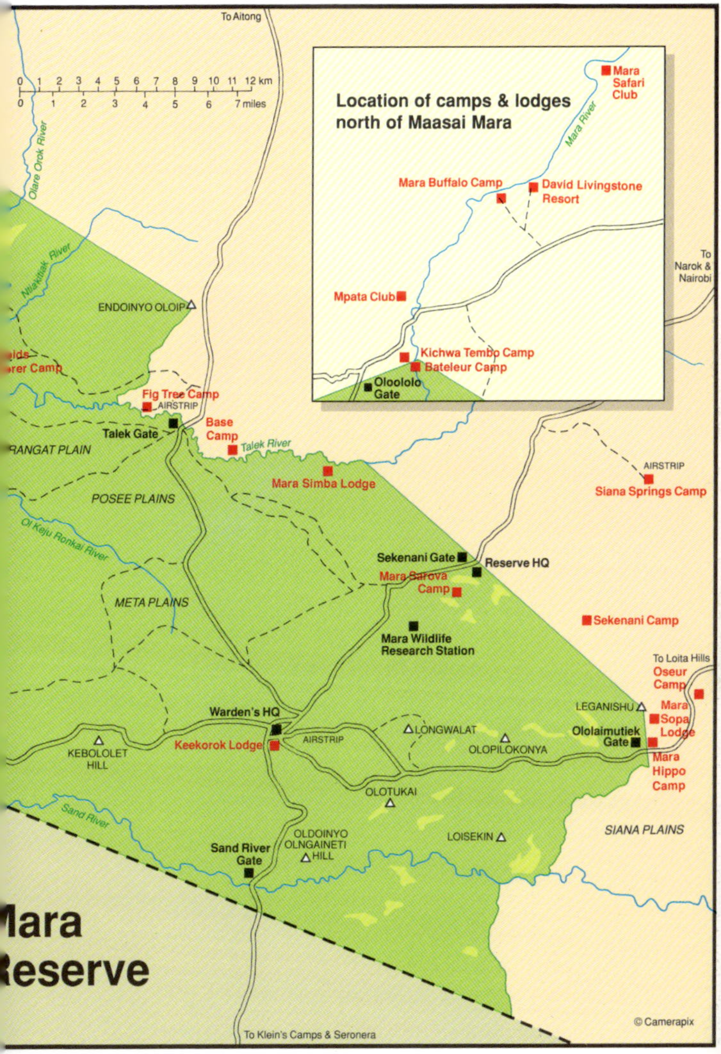

Location of camps & lodges north of Maasai Mara
Mara Safari Club
Mara River
Mara Buffalo Camp
David Livingstone Resort
Mpata Club
Kichwa Tembo Camp
Bateleur Camp
Oloololo Gate
To Narok & Nairobi
To Aitong
0 1 2 3 4 5 6 7 8 9 10 11 12 km
0 1 2 3 4 5 6 7 miles
Olare Orok River
Ntiakitiak River
ENDOINYO OLOIP
Fig Tree Camp
AIRSTRIP
Talek Gate
Base Camp
Talek River
Mara Simba Lodge
POSEE PLAINS
Ol Keju Ronkai River
META PLAINS
Sekenani Gate
Reserve HQ
Mara Sarova Camp
Mara Wildlife Research Station
AIRSTRIP
Siana Springs Camp
Sekenani Camp
To Loita Hills
Oseur Camp
LEGANISHU
Mara Sopa Lodge
Ololaimutiek Gate
Mara Hippo Camp
Warden's HQ
Keekorok Lodge
AIRSTRIP
LONGWALAT
OLOPILOKONYA
KEBOLOLET HILL
OLOTUKAI
Sand River
Sand River Gate
OLDOINYO OLNGAINETI HILL
LOISEKIN
SIANA PLAINS
ara Reserve
© Camerapix
To Klein's Camps & Seronera

1. The empty Land

It is probable that the Maasai people first entered the Serengeti-Mara area in the mid-eighteenth century. For more than 200 years the Mara at least, and much of the Serengeti, has been accepted as Maasailand. The land would have been sparsely populated; the nomadic lifestyle of the Maasai meant that the great herds of cattle would move wherever grass and water were available. There was ample room for humans and wildlife to coexist, neither impinging on the interests of the other.

By the end of the 19th century, Maasai fortunes were at an ebb. Around the early 1880s there had been prolonged drought. The already weakened herds of cattle were then hit by an epidemic of the bovine disease *pleuropneumonia*, for which, in those days, there was no cure. Large numbers of cattle succumbed and the Maasai suffered massive losses.

A few years later fresh disaster struck. The killer disease rinder-pest made its appearance, carried by domestic stock introduced by alien adventurers and settlers. The deadly cattle virus spread quickly, killing vast numbers of African cattle and wiping out equally large numbers of buffalo and wildebeest. Until the early 1950s, when a campaign to immunise cattle against the disease begun, periodic outbreaks occurred keeping the wildebeest population down to about 250,000 animals. As immunisation became more widespread, an unexpected disappearance of rinderpest among the buffalo and wildebeest was noticed. An indication, virtual proof in fact, that it was the cattle infecting the wildlife, and not the other way round, as many in authority chose to believe.

By the mid-1890s the Maasai had lost at least 95 per cent of their stock, their only wealth and source of livelihood. As if this were not enough, smallpox and internecine clan warfare took further toll on human lives and by 1900 the Maasai were a decimated, scattered people, concentrated close to

The empty Land

the newly-developing centres of population like Nairobi, having left most of their traditional grazing grounds.

About the same time, elephant populations were much reduced through hunting, a consequence of the flourishing slave trade. It worked well for the traders – the captured slaves could carry the ivory to the coast to make the long and hazardous trip doubly worthwhile.

The Serengeti-Mara was largely empty of stock and wildlife, in the form of elephant, buffalo and wildebeest, and of people. At that time the area was described by early visitors – missionaries, hunters and administrators – as, 'fine open grass country, some brush, but not much' and 'open, grassy, rolling, country'. Not so very different, you may think, from what is seen today, and you are probably right.

So, by 1900 or so, with elephant numbers greatly reduced by the slave traders' hunting; wildebeest and buffalo by rinderpest; the Maasai by famine and disease, and their cattle herds virtually wiped out, the plains and open grass country were spared the heavy grazing and browsing of domestic stock and large herbivores, and the annual fires set by humans. Thus a process of bush and woodland recovery began.

Some 30 or so years later, as the European hunters and administrators began to take a closer interest in the Mara and to consider her value as a potential natural resource, the area had become much more wooded. Many of the previously grassy plains were covered with well-established stands of acacia and thick bush. Thickets grew on the hilltops and the now thickly wooded country housed an enormously diverse and abundant population of wildlife.

As the woodlands became more established they began to provide a perfect habitat for the tsetse fly, *Glossina swynnertoni*, which transmits Sleeping Sickness in man and trypanosomiasis in cattle. The tsetse needs thick bush

Adult and young at a Mara waterhole. Like humans, elephants enjoy physical touch and social contact.

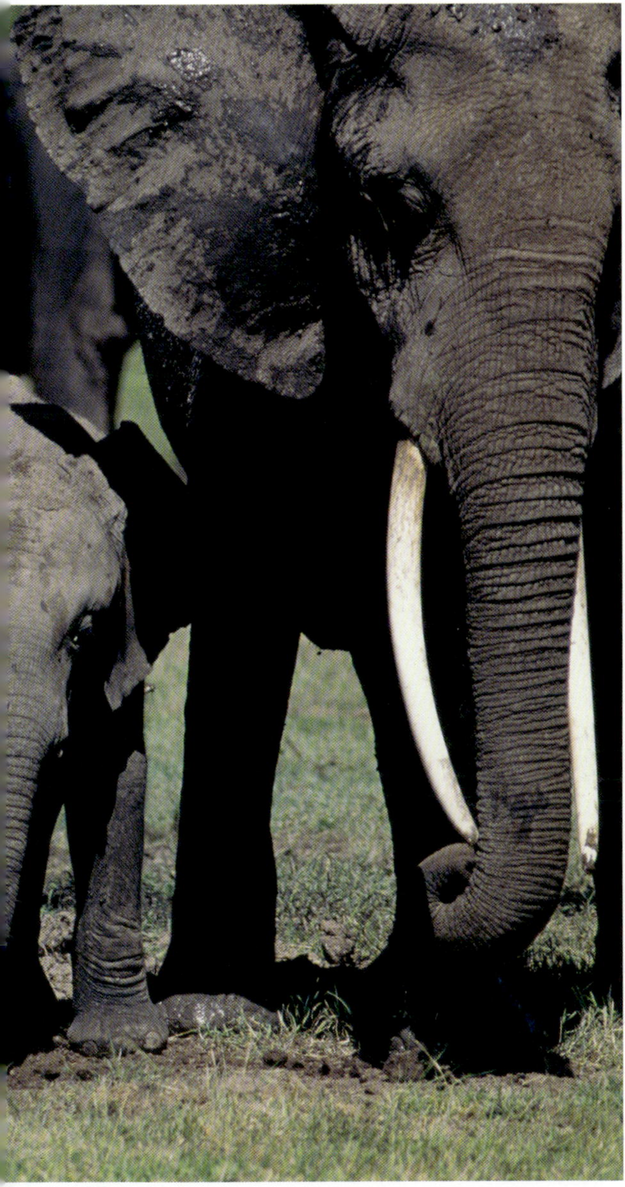

The empty Land

to survive and, while wild animals are largely immune to its transmitted diseases, domestic cattle and humans are not. The establishment of tsetse in large numbers rendered the area virtually uninhabitable to man and his stock.

It is remarkable how quickly Africa's grasslands revert to woodland. In Uganda's Murchison Falls National Park, where rainfall is similar to the Mara, following the elimination of elephant in the 1970s, large areas of grassland became woodland, six to 10 metres high, within six years. A similar ecological change almost certainly occurred in the Serengeti-Mara in the wake of the rinderpest epidemic. Since the Maasai Mara was comparatively little known until perhaps the mid-1930s, it is not surprising that as it became more widely visited it was assumed that what the new wave of Mara travellers saw was the true, pristine state of the Serengeti-Mara ecosystem.

There were early moves to preserve this newly discovered paradise, teeming with wildlife and apparently uninhabited and unclaimed by indigenous peoples. Since it was so magnificently untamed many could not bear to think of agricultural or human development spoiling what was seen as untouched Africa. However, there were just as many who cast covetous eyes upon the fertile land, seeing it as ripe for settlement and the ripping plough, and as neat, fenced paddocks for prime beef cattle.

Tanganyika (as Tanzania then was) so often ahead of the field in those days, led the way by declaring the Serengeti a Game Reserve in 1930, with no hunting permitted. It was elevated to National Park status in the late 1940s. Not until after the Second World War did Kenya follow suit, creating the Mara Game Reserve in 1948. This was an area some 518 square kilometres in extent to the west of the Mara River, the area referred to today as the Mara Triangle. It was not until 1961 that the Maasai Mara National Reserve came into being.

The empty Land

Serious work to tackle the tsetse problem had begun in the early 1950s, mainly in the form of bush-clearing and the attempted elimination of wildlife hosts. The schemes were expensive and largely unsuccessful. Well into the 1960s the game reserve and areas adjacent to it were occupied by the Maasai during exceptionally dry conditions. The success of the rinder-pest immunisation campaigns meant the Maasai herds began to increase. Improved medical coverage for the Maasai, even in the remotest areas, meant lower infant mortality rates and a greater life expectation for adults. With increased numbers of people and their cattle, there came increased pressure on grazing lands to the north. This was aggravated by a steady influx of non-Maasai settlers who were more inclined to cultivation than their hosts, and these combined factors precipitated a gradual drift southward in search of grazing. At the same time, development (or destruction as some prefer to describe it) of the Mau forest range further restricted dry season grazing for sheep and goats.

Increased human presence and activity brought increased burning to clear bush and encourage a new flush of grass. Trees and thickets were felled for housing and firewood. Inevitably the bush gave way and the tsetse retreated. This attracted more herders, and it became clear that if something were not done the whole area would be settled and occupied by stock, and – even worse – come under the plough.

Bush clearing was assisted by an unexpected rise in the numbers of elephant. While elephant had always been present throughout the Serengeti-Mara, movements were generally seasonal, and the numbers of permanent residents were never particularly high. The reason for the rise in numbers kept the minds of researchers and game department officials occupied for a long time. However, the most likely answer is that a rising human population, agricultural development and consequent fencing and

An elephant herd at a Mara waterhole.

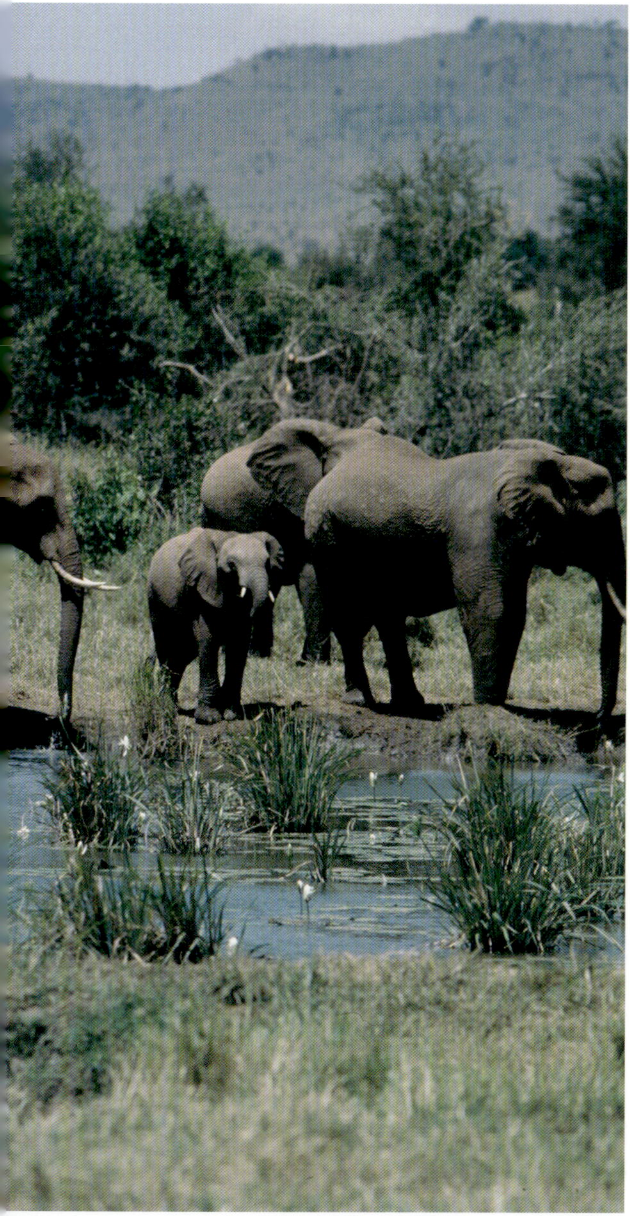

The empty Land

housing probably disturbed traditional migration routes, and succeeding generations of elephant adapted to change, became more sedentary and, like the Maasai, less nomadic.

As the attempts to eradicate tsetse were abandoned, after enormous expense, the colonial government, with rare foresight and determination, embarked on a campaign to create a conservation area as a permanent wildlife sanctuary. While questions were raised over the validity of the claim of the Maasai to the Mara, the authorities were never in doubt. Kenya's early political history shows that the claim was valid, and that the task facing the authorities was one of persuasion.

Whatever the human and political impact on conservation, nature has one great leveller up her sleeve drought. Science may pull aside the curtain that hides many of the mysteries of the wild; research may help in ridding the world of irritants such as tsetse; management techniques may preserve, even improve, wildlife numbers and their habitat but science has yet to master the climate.

The years 1961 and 1984 were years of severe drought, when wild animals, especially buffalo, perished in large numbers. The Maasai suffered terrible hunger and loss of cattle. As animals died, vegetation withered and streams dried up and the hopes of naturalists and conservationists were dashed. It seemed that the land would never recover, that the animals and vegetation would be so reduced it would leave the Mara a wasteland. But when rain fell at last, recovery was swift. Vegetation flourished; young animals were born and within a year or two the herds filled the grasslands as if the tragedies of previous months were but a passing episode in the Mara's ecological history – which of course it was. Drought again visited the Mara in 1993 and 2006. This time the toll seemed greater. Hippos, which require vast amounts of greenery, died in large numbers. The rotting carcasses of buffalo and antelope littered the plains.

The empty Land

Each successive drought creates a subtle change – a tree gone here, a patch of bush there.

And so it seems the ecological circle is complete. The Maasai Mara is again open grassland, with fewer thickets and woodlands, wrought by an invincible triumvirate – man, elephant and fire. There has been a massive decline in woodland cover in the past five decades, and change continues. Despite our knowledge, mankind can be certain of nothing where nature is concerned. Admittedly, nature does get a little help from mankind and the ability to monitor ecological change makes the present and future of greater concern than the past.

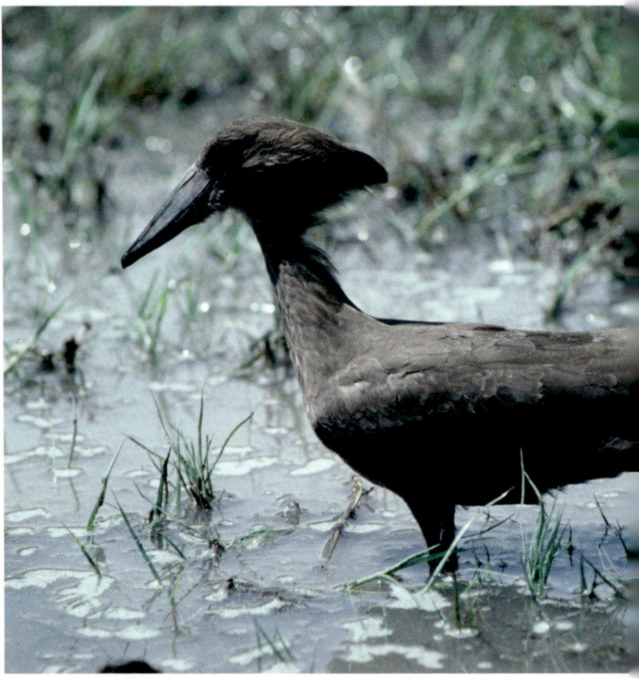

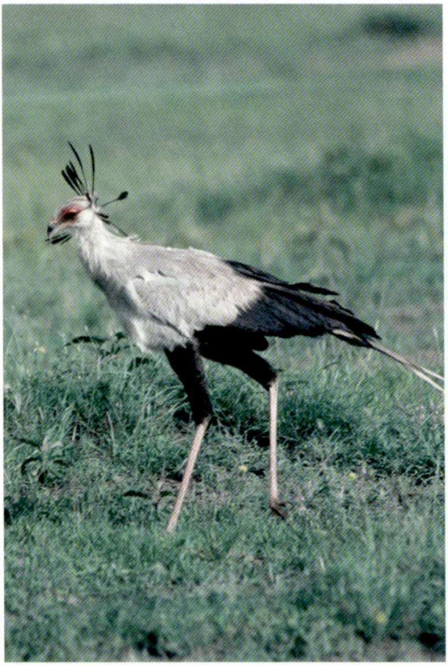

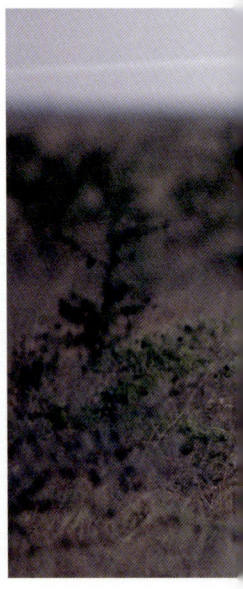

Left: **Hamerkop** – which has one of the heaviest nests in the bird kingdom.

Opposite bottom: **Secretary Bird**. A raptor, the species feeds primarily on snakes.

Below: **Crowned Crane** – National symbol of Uganda – are common in the Maasai Mara.

2. The making of a Game Reserve

Until the early part of the 20th century, Kenya, as a separate country, did not exist. British colonial interest centred on Uganda. Control of the headwaters of the Nile meant control of Egypt and the Suez Canal – the British Empire's lifeline. Realising that supplying the new Uganda Protectorate's garrison through the Nile was costly and cumbersome, the British decided to build a railway from Mombasa to Uganda. The protectorate's boundary ran close to the eastern wall of the Rift Valley, with Naivasha the nearest outpost to the coast. Work on the railway began in mid-1895 and in December 1901 the first train reached Kisumu, on the shore of Lake Victoria. Early in 1902 the eastern part of Uganda, from the lake to Naivasha, was transferred to the East Africa Protectorate, administered from the newly established railway town of Nairobi.

At that time Africa's wildlife was largely taken for granted. To Kenya's indigenous people wild animals were nothing remarkable, for who was to know that other countries were not similarly blessed? To the newcomers – railwaymen, traders, missionaries and adventurers – the numbers of wildlife seemed unlimited. Few gave thought to the future.

At the turn of the century, however, a minority of far-sighted people realised that some control and certain policies ware needed if wildlife was to survive the pressures imposed by settlement and development.

There were early signs that the numbers of some species were in decline. So, in 1899, two huge game reserves were created, the northern and the southern, which virtually made the whole of Kenya one vast game reserve. A Game Ranger, equivalent to Chief Game Warden in later years, was appointed in 1901, and the Game Department, was established in 1906 to administer the newly introduced game laws.

These early measures, i.e. limiting the numbers of animals shot and protecting the rarer species, were aimed largely at the prevention of poaching and the control of hunting for sport.

The making of a Game Reserve

Concern for the conservation of their habitat came much later as there was still plenty of room fir wild animals and people. As settlements and the African population increased, more land was cleared with an inevitable decline in several animal species. Many were eliminated deliberately – by farmers and as government policy. Lion, for example, which were a menace to stock farmers, were frequently poisoned and treated as vermin. Only in sparsely populated areas, such as Maasailand, did wild animals – neither a source of food nor of conflict – survive in large numbers.

Nairobi National Park, the first national park in Kenya, was established in 1945, on the fringes of the developing city. It was followed by the Tsavo Parks in 1948 and in subsequent years there were additions, including the formation of marine parks at the coast.

There is a legal and technical difference between a national park and a national reserve. A national park is an area set aside and taken over by government for the exclusive purpose of preserving wildlife and its habitat. Human activity is excluded, except under strictly controlled conditions and the park is run by the country's supreme wildlife authority – the Kenya Wildlife Service. A national reserve, however, is usually run by a local government authority for the benefit of the local people. It is protected by council by-laws, and human activity is not necessarily excluded.

No country, let alone one in Africa, can afford to set aside vast tracts of land for the sole purpose of preserving wild animals. So a policy of developing national parks and reserves was launched. This included the construction of lodges and camps to accommodate the growing number of tourists who were beginning to take a keen interest in Africa (especially Kenya), their enthusiasm for observing wildlife in a natural environment greatly fuelled by television. After all, wildlife had to bring in economic rewards to justify the land secured for its own protection.

The making of a Game Reserve

Slowly the realisation dawned that protecting the animals was but a part of the necessary strategy to establish a credible tourism industry. Protecting the habitat and safe-guarding the sometimes-fragile soil structure, water supplies and vegetation from degradation was also important. As was creating areas that not just offered wildlife spectacles, but also served as valuable conservation units in which all of nature was preserved in harmony. No park or reserve can ever be a completely self-sufficient system. Few are fenced or have visible boundaries. Animals were free, and to a remarkable extent still are, to migrate along traditional routes.

This leads to one of Kenya's major conservation problems. The cost of fencing every park or reserve would be enormous. Such a move would drastically alter the traditional concept of wildlife conservation, and would create units similar to safari parks found in developed countries. The attraction of Kenya and East Africa has been the fact that wild animals roam free, and that apart from the intensively farmed areas of the Western and Central Provinces, a traveller is likely to see wildlife grazing close to main roads and in the countryside. Adequate safeguards must be found in unprotected areas to which animals migrate when those areas cannot be integrated into the park or reserve concerned. Wildlife management, as opposed to the administration of parks, increasingly preoccupies the minds of those entrusted with the task of implementing conservation policy.

The Maasai Mara is a national reserve, not a national park, and powerful social and political reasons suggest it is unlikely to become one in the immediate future. The reserve came into being in 1961, after some two years hard bargaining between the Maasai people and the then colonial government. When professional and private game hunting in Kenya was outlawed in mid-1977, no hunting had been permitted for many years in the Mara area, though limited licences were granted for shooting around its limits.

The making of a Game Reserve

From the first efforts at conserving the Mara, which began in the early 1960s, wildlife has proliferated – with steady increases in the herds of plains game and elephant.

There are two hazards faced by those who administer the parks. The first is fire. Whether a fire starts outside the park and spreads into it, or whether it started within park boundaries, a fire in the dry season is extremely difficult to control. Many parks and reserves adopt a policy of controlled burning, set for a certain time of year (usually after rain), when a 'cool' burn will take out dead grass and other vegetation, and encourage a fresh crop of grass without damaging trees or established bush. Effective firebreaks are expensive to construct and sadly the Mara has suffered for many years from uncontrolled burning. Fires, often lit outside, sweep their remorseless way through great tracts of bush, causing irreparable damage.

The second habitat hazard is caused by the animals themselves. As more animals concentrate within a park, driven there by the dangers of the surrounding areas, they multiply without hindrance. Over-population of animals can lead to destruction of the vegetation to the extent where it can no longer support either the animals responsible, or any other species. It is no longer possible to cling to the philosophy that flora and fauna in a national park or reserve should be left for nature to regulate. With animals confined more and more within a limited space eating themselves out of house and home and with what remains devoured by fire, it is a miracle that anything survives. This then is the Maasai Mara. Aided by a generous rainfall, not only does it survive all these pressures, it also survives a third hazard – the motor vehicle. The popularity of the Mara attracts a greater vehicle density than any other park. That the Mara not just survives, but flourishes, is a tribute to the resilience of the land, its remarkable ability to recover from the abuse heaped upon it by man, and the wildlife which adapts so successfully to changing environmental conditions.

Above: **Aerial view of a hippo haunt in the Mara River.**

Opposite right: **Monitor Lizard – a primeval species that abounds in the Maasai Mara.**

Right: **Hippos congregate at deep bends in the Mara River.**

31

3. The Maasai People

To the early explorers the Maasai people were greatly feared, and seen as a fierce people who not only barred progress to the hinterland but also raided other tribes and each other for cattle.

They occupied vast tracts of East Africa. Nomadic, moving frequently over large distances to follow grazing and water, they held sway virtually throughout present day Kenya. Their aggression confined many tribes, such as the Kikuyu, to forest areas and high ground. The early caravans were prepared to pay tribute to secure passage through Maasai-controlled lands, while other less influential people were overcome by force or guile.

The Kenyan Maasai were separated from the rest of the East African Maasai by the imposition of a political boundary, drawn from the coast to Lake Victoria, following the Berlin Conference of 1895. Kenya came under British rule and the south was handed to Germany. It was known as German East Africa until after World War I when the territory's administration was mandated to Britain by the League of Nations, and the country became Tanganyika.

The Kenyan Maasai were subjected to a series of agreements and treaties with the colonial government to limit raiding and allow European settlement. While the Maasai were held in great respect by the government, little compunction was shown in imposing the treaties. Through the 1904 treaty, the Northern and Southern Maasai Reserves were created. In 1911 a subsequent treaty forced the Maasai to abandon the Northern or Laikipia Reserve and settle south of the 'Uganda Railway' line. This agreement was later challenged in the High Court but the case was lost, as was the appeal that followed.

Having contained the Maasai, the colonial government was content thereafter to leave them to lead their traditional and conservative way of life. This policy was helped by the people's apparent acquiescence and desire to be left alone and not

The Maasai People

hastened into accepting new technology. Progress in education, livestock management and water supplies was slow.

The Maasai did not lose their natural enthusiasm for stock theft. They took every opportunity to raid neighbouring African people, European farms and each other for cattle. The 'moran' system encouraged stock theft. Young men, after circumcision at about fifteen years old, were gathered as a military wing in the moran *manyatta* – a form of barracks – and would stay together for the next five or so years. A graduation ceremony disbanded the moran before the next age grade took over. It was inevitable that a large group of fit, virile young men would find time on their hands. Stealing cattle, for pride and on which to feast, was an obvious outlet for pent-up energy. The administration was mainly preoccupied with resolving such thefts, either by tracking the perpetrators and bringing them to court, or through lengthy border committee negotiations to agree compensation. In the early 1980s the Narok Maasai abolished the moran system, and the elegant but scantily clad red-ochred young men carrying polished spears are no longer seen.

The succession of treaties and forced moves from traditional lands left the Maasai with an inherited reluctance to enter into any negotiation that might deprive them of more. While Maasailand teemed with game, suggestions that the southern part, infested with tsetse fly and apparently useless for stock and human habitation be turned into a national park were met with spirited resistance.

It was more than a question of not wanting the animals. The Maasai have a long tradition of tolerance of and co-existence with wildlife. Though generations have grumbled about the competition for grazing from wild herbivores, zebra and wildebeest in particular, wild animals have generally never been hunted for food. However, wildlife was far from ignored. Senior Government Zoologist Dr. Phil Glover compiled an ecological survey of the Mara area

Maasai warriors perform traditional jumping, standing-still dance.

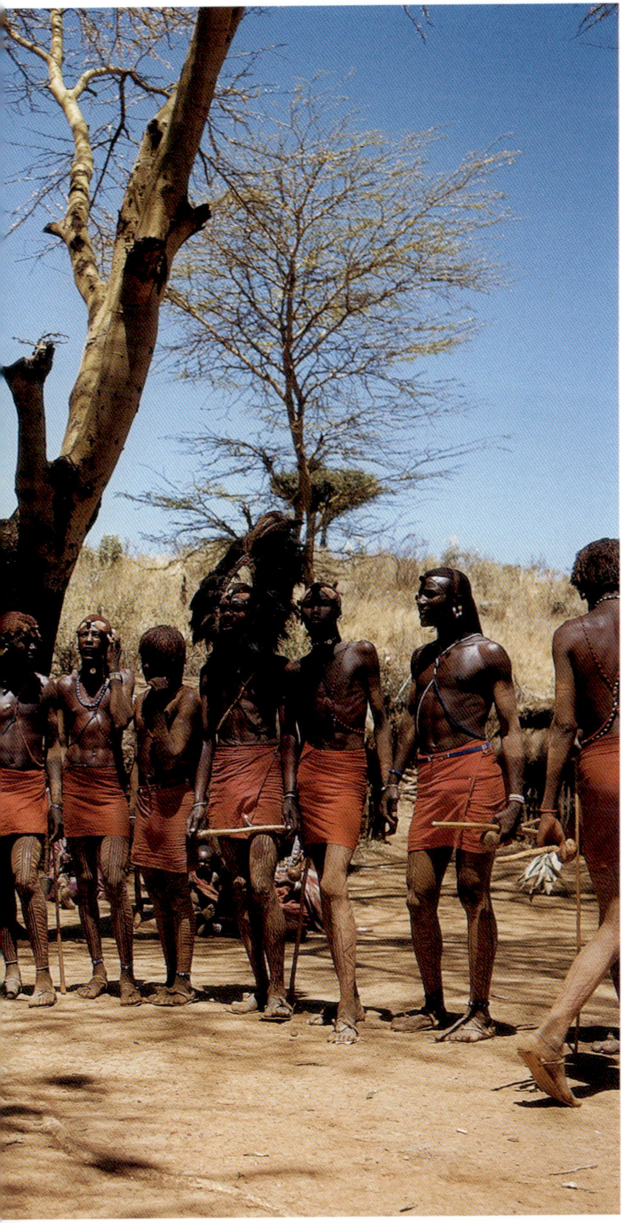

The Maasai People

in 1962. At that time I was a District Officer in Narok and contributed a review of Maasai attitudes to wild animals. Originally the purpose was to find out to what extent the Maasai were 'natural naturalists'. It was prompted by the fact that they had a name for every animal and tree and for most birds. The work yielded many interesting facts.

While the Maasai would not hunt wildlife for food, they were happy to drive lion and other predators away from eland or giraffe kills and take away the meat. Giraffe tails were keenly sought as fly whisks (*olkweteti*); buffalo hide for war shields; impala and Colobus monkey skins for ceremonial clothing. Many animals provided medicines for man and beast. Others provided ornaments, weapons, ropes and thongs. Several animals had a cultural significance or were regarded as omens. A hedgehog, for instance, was a bringer of good luck, provided the right ritual was followed. It had to be carried home and left overnight in the cattle enclosure. The next day it was allowed to go free. It must never be killed or harmed. On the other hand, Maasai belief is that the African hare brings great misfortune. Should a hare run between a man's leg – even worse a woman's – it is a portent of misfortune, even death. Purification has to take place immediately. A sheep is slaughtered, some of its stomach contents are spilt over the ground where the incident happened, and some on the inner thighs of the victim.

The Maasai dislike most predators. Though the lion may be respected for its strength and intelligence, it is seen as a menace to cattle. Outside the game reserve, the killing of lion either by spear or chemical cattle dip is commonplace. Cheetah, too, are regarded less than sympathetically by shepherds and goatherds. The wild dog now locally extinct, and the jackal are detested and seen as fair game when close to domestic stock. There has always been resentment of the wildebeest, which compete for grazing with Maasai cattle. The resentment has grown during the last forty years. The migration seen today

The Maasai People

is a comparatively recent phenomenon. Until the early 1970s there was little evidence of such migration. Only after the elimination of rinder-pest and an increase in dry season rainfall (which caused an astonishing increase in numbers) did the wildebeest migration began to spill over from the Serengeti into the Mara. With no sign of a reduction in numbers, the migration now spreads beyond the game reserve to the surrounding lands, where the plough and extensive wheat growing schemes have taken over much traditional grazing land, forcing the cattle to retreat.

With a changing pattern in land tenure, where the tradition of communally owned land is rapidly giving way to the demarcation of registered individual holdings, resentment towards competing wild herbivores only becomes greater, and demands for the control of invading wildlife more strident and insistent. While successful tourism depends on the abundance of wildlife, successful farming demands the opposite. So the long, apparent harmony between the Maasai and the wildlife is now uneasy. Somehow a compromise must be found. In an age of compromise one almost certainly will, albeit at a price.

The basis for such compromise already exists. The first move to preserve wildlife in Maasailand was made in 1948, when the 518-square-kilometre Mara Triangle was declared a game reserve. Later, the area east of the Mara River, known locally as the 'fly area', became a game control area with limited hunting. In 1954, lion, leopard, cheetah and rhino were given total protection. By the end of the 1950s the entire area had been closed to hunting, and access was granted only to photographic parties. The next move was the expansion of the closed areas to form a much larger comprehensive game reserve, owned and managed by the Maasai themselves, and run as a commercial enterprise.

The architect of the imaginative scheme was Major Evelyn Temple-Boreham, Senior game Warden, Narok.

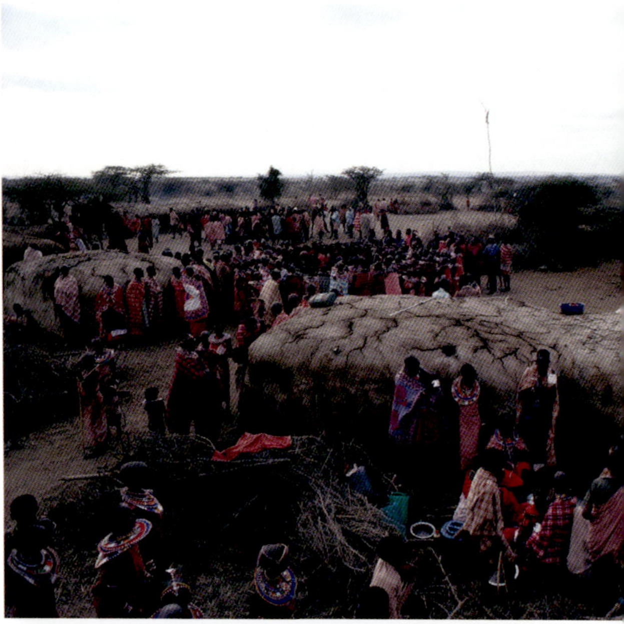

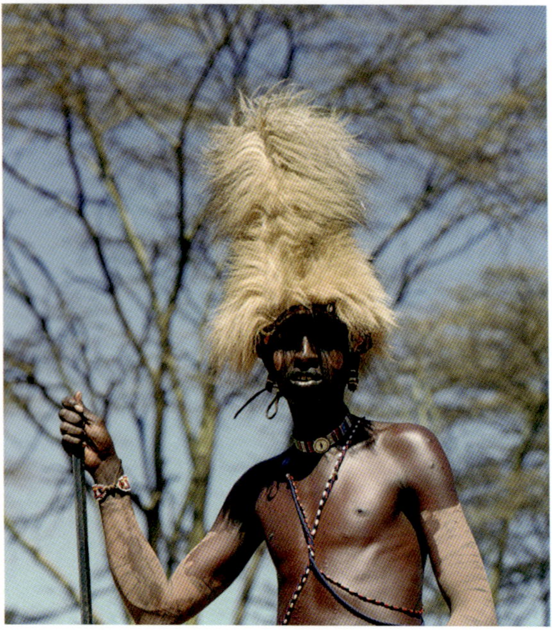

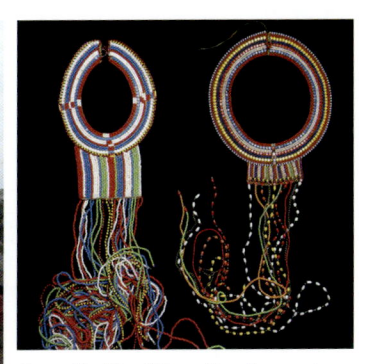

Above: Traditional Maasai jewellery made from brightly coloured beadwork.

Left: Crowds gather early in the morning awaiting the arrival of the moran after the warriors' night vigil.

Opposite bottom: Maasai warrior with lion mane headdress, symbol that he has speared a lion to death.

Below: Young Maasai maiden decked out in traditional finery.

The Maasai People

A pragmatist to his toenails TB, as he was universally known, served most of his working life in the Mara. He went there as Game Ranger before World War II, and rose in rand and stature, refusing promotion and transfer. Although he acted as Chief Game Warden, based in Nairobi for short periods, he was happier in the Mara and owned no ambitions for higher office.

He may have been an old-fashioned martinet, a stickler for enforcing the game laws on professional hunters, yet he was sympathetic to the Ndorobo, a small section of forest-dwelling Maasai who lived by hunting and by gathering fruit and honey. He was prepared to turn a blind eye to their hunting provided it was simply for food, and that they did not kill elephant, rhino or lion for commercial gain.

Early on, TB was convinced that any long-term policy to preserve wildlife would succeed only if the people who either owned or claimed the land could benefit directly. He foresaw the pressures that could arise and, indeed, have. With tremendous determination and tenacity he set out to convince the Maasai that they should build on the existing preservation measures and establish their own game reserve, which they would control to exploit the tourism industry beginning to take shape, moving away from big game hunting to photography and the appreciation of nature. Eco-tourism, today's phrase, hadn't been coined then but, more than thirty years ago, TB perceived its advent.

Given the traditional Maasai sensitivity on matters concerning land, for which they have good reason, it was an ambitious undertaking. The Maasai had already spurned substantial financial offers from the government to accept the creation of a national park. It took two years of patient negotiation and hard bargaining, but the trust and respect in which Temple-Boreham was held was such that he finally won through. The Maasai Mara National Reserve, slightly larger than it is today – owned, managed and administered

The Maasai People

by the Narok County Council (the local government authority for the area) – came into being.

Such an arrangements not meet with universal approval. For long, a formidable body of opinion has wanted the Mara under central control, administered by successive wildlife bodies within the national park system. Yet, while the national parks were deteriorating under poor management in the 1970s and early 1980s, and reeling from a wave of unprecedented and unlimited poaching, the Maasai Mara developed its reputation and its facilities to become the most visited wildlife destination in East Africa. Indeed the only Mara animal to suffer, to any significant extent, from the two decades of relentless poaching was the rhino, brought almost to elimination.

This then, may be the compromise needed. If the Maasai Mara continues to flourish, to attract visitors and to maintain its reputation as one of the greatest wildlife sanctuaries in the world, it will continue to be an important resource for the Maasai people. Although wild animals may be less tolerated on farms, the vast numbers could be exploited, especially during the spectacular wildebeest migration. There is probably as much future for wildlife, as an exploitable resource, on private land as in the parks and formal Reserves.

Within the formal game reserve, and on private land outside, there are several well-appointed lodges and camps, which provide a standard of accommodation and facilities to satisfy the most fastidious visitor. As more land becomes owned individually, and enclosed, it must be expected that the new landowners will seek to develop their own attractions for visitors and set up campsites. Facilities within the so-called 'group ranch' areas are becoming increasingly high quality and well-organised and the professional safari firms run exceptionally well-organised, and indeed luxurious, mobile tented camps in the traditional style.

TB died in 1969 but the Maasai Mara is a living memorial to his life's work.

4. The Mara Country

In Maa, the Maasai language, mara means spotted, and is used sometimes to refer to, or describe, the leopard – *olowuaru mara*, the spotted wild animal. Seen from high ground, the effect of stream, thicket and open ground is not unlike the dappled coat of a giant leopard or cheetah. Flowing from the Mau Forest, the waters of the Mara River only take their name after they have been joined by the Amala and Nyangoris rivers, before they reach Maasailand. The Maasai call the river *enkare dapash* – meaning wide stream – or *enkipai*, the meaning of which is more involved. Literally *enkipai* means the slime on newborn children or animals, and is often used as a form of blessing – *taa inkipa!* – meaning become blessed. It may be used as a girl's name, Noonkipa, the one of the slime or of good blessings. So with a little imagination the Mara River becomes the 'River of Good Fortune'.

The most common grass is the Red Oat Grass (*Themeda triandra*). Its russet seed heads, rather like an oat head, hence the popular name, give the Mara grassland its distinctive brownish look at dry times of the year. Among the red oat grass, clumps of a darker grass stand tall, waving in the mid-day breeze. This is *Hyparrhenia*, useful elsewhere for thatching. After burning, even before rain, the red oat grass puts out new shoots and, always palatable, is eagerly sought out by the plains gazelle and antelope.

A popular food plant for the black rhinoceros is the Sodom Apple, *Solanum icanum*, a smallish low-growing shrub with purple flowers and round yellow fruit, common in the open plain. The dominant bush is the distinctive *Croton dichogamus*. Growing in thickets, some extending over several acres, its smooth leaves, with a silver tinge below, turn reddish with age and provide shade in the heat of the day for many animals. It has little attraction as a food plant, though elephants will strip the branches for the capsule fruit.

The Mara Country

The woodlands are predominantly acacia and, of the seven or so species in the Mara, one of the most distinctive is the yellow Fever Tree, *Acacia xanthlophloea*. With its flat top and yellow, powdery bark, it is usually found along watercourses, and takes its name from its association with malaria and damp places. The branches, especially when the small yellow or pinkish flowers are in bloom, hum with activity – busy with bees, and small birds feeding and courting (the tree is much favoured by many of the sunbird family). The upper branches may provide a viewpoint for an aristocratic avian raptor, a fish eagle perhaps, keeping a sharp eye out for prey. In the Seronera area of the Serengeti, the lower branches are favourite spots for leopard basking in the early morning sun.

An unusual acacia, which stands stunted and shrubby rather than tall and flat-topped like most species, is the Whistling Thorn, *Acacia drepanolobium*, which grows on the black cotton soil of the plains. It has numerous galls that harden and turn black with age. These are inhabited by small ants with a painful sting. Any disturbance, such as a giraffe attempting to browse the leaves, brings out the ants – bent on vengeance. The raider soon moves on. Each gall occupied by the ants has two small holes set either side. When the wind blows through these, it sets up a tiny whistling sound, which is quite noticeable when a whole clump is in full cry.

The low-branched German Sausage Tree, *Kigelia aethopium*, has sausage-like fruit, one to three feet long and about four inches thick, hanging from its branches rather like a continental delicatessen. The fruit may be used to flavour home-brewed beer, and rhino feed on the windfalls. The maroon flowers have a nasty smell, which doesn't seem to deter the nectar-seeking sunbirds. It is a good shade tree and campers will often pitch a tent under its spreading branches.

Above: Lion cubs sit under the branches of a shady tree away from the intense heat of the midday sun.

Opposite: Marabou storks rest on the boughs of an acacia tree at sunset.

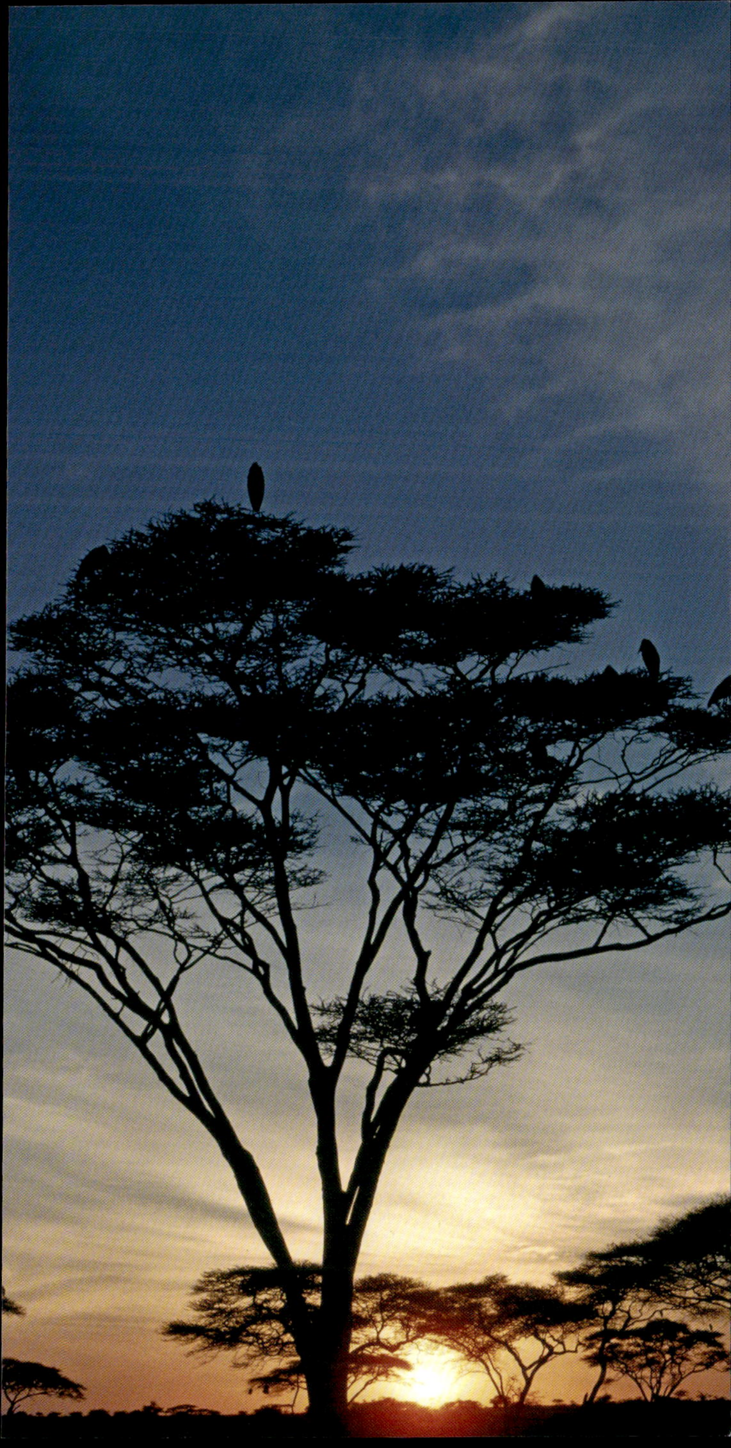

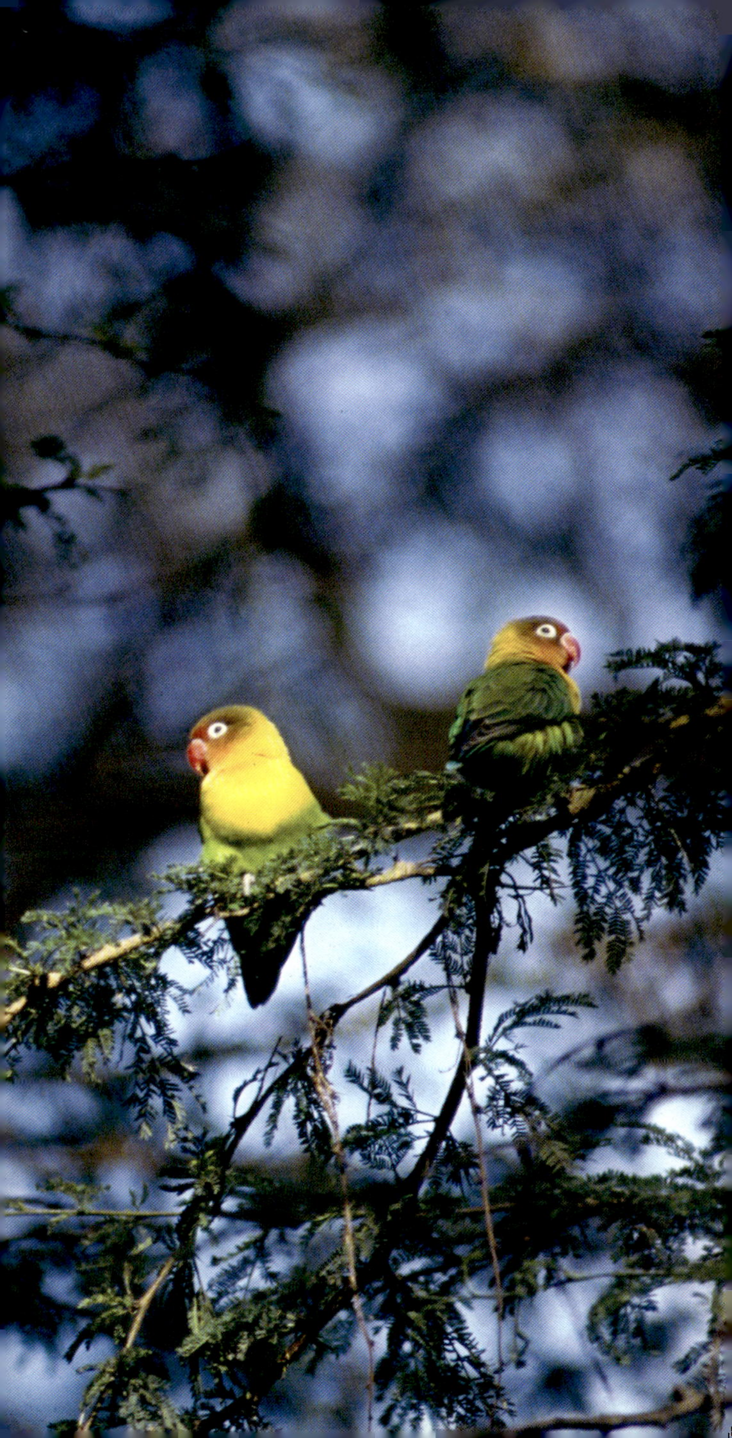

Above: Water lilies.

Opposite: Two love-birds alight on an acacia bough.

Left: *Gloriosa superba* Lily, locally known as 'Flame lily'.

The Mara Country

On your travels you will see lone, erect trees with flat tops, often housing a large, untidy nest that could belong to the secretary bird or vulture. This is the Desert Date, *Balanites aegyptiaca*. The small, yellow flowers turn to a ripe, yellow fruit with a large, hard, pointed stone surrounded by sticky but edible flesh. The kernel yields over forty per cent of oil, sometimes called zachun oil, believed to have been an ingredient of the spikenard mentioned in the Christian scriptures. The fruit has other uses. An emulsion made from it is lethal to the freshwater snails that act as intermediary hosts for *bilharzia*, a debilitating disease common in Africa. The emulsion is also lethal to the water-flea that carries Guinea-worm disease, the eradication of which occupied much of the energy of former American president, Jimmy Carter.

The acacias provide food for elephants, baboons and gazelles. Elephant will strip the bark of favoured trees and reach high for the seedpods, also sought by the baboon. Pods that fall to the ground are eagerly snapped up by impala and small rodents. In a mysterious way, it seems that passing through an elephant's digestive system helps many acacia seeds to germinate – an important contribution to the regeneration of the creature's food supply.

Stands of trees along the river banks, or those that form copses out on the plains, often display a distinct and regular line some six metres or so above the ground, almost as if pruned with a pair of garden shears. This is the giraffe browse line, and represents the limit of their reach.

Among the varied trees that fringe the riverbanks, the East African Greenheart, *Warburgia ugandensis*, stands out. Though some grow to more than 40 metres high, mature trees are more usually about 30 metres tall. The fruit, on which pigeons and baboons feed, is hard and green. The timber has a high oil content and, when used for a campfire, burns with an incense-like smell. The greenheart is

The Mara Country

generally accompanied by stands of African Wild Olive, *Olea africana*, olioirien in Maa – the timber of which was once used in large quantities to fuel railway steam engines. The slender *Diospyros abyssinica* is interspersed with clumps of the Wild Date Palm, Phoenix reclinata, makindu in Swahili – the fronds of which are widely used for passable toddy.

The Mara River is the major watercourse in the area. Of several smaller rivers and streams, the most important is the Sand river, which forms a rough southern boundary with neighbouring Tanzania. As the name implies, for much of the year, the river appears to consist of sand with but a trickle of flowing water. But there is water close to the surface and only a little digging is needed to reach it – as elephant well know. At other times of the year, it flows with majestic fury to join the Mara below the southern bridge – sweeping before it the carcasses of wildebeest who cross the waters in their thousands, in an apparent lunatic frenzy to return to their southerly migration route.

It is remarkable for such a large mass and variety of grazing animals to survive in such a comparatively small area as the Maasai Mara Game Reserve (roughly 1,500 square kilometres). There are two contributory factors. The first is that they can migrate southward to the Serengeti, where the wildebeest return after their four or five months sojourn, or to the north on to private land where, by and large, they are still tolerated. The second factor is what is known generally as the grazing succession. The heavy grazers, the elephant, buffalo and hippo, eat and trample the long, coarse grasses and bring about change that makes the grass palatable to the lighter grazers, the zebra, wildebeest and larger antelope (hartebeest, topi, eland), who in turn reduce the vegetation to suit the lightest grazers of all, Grant's and Thomson's gazelle, and the warthog, who spend most of their feeding time on their knees.

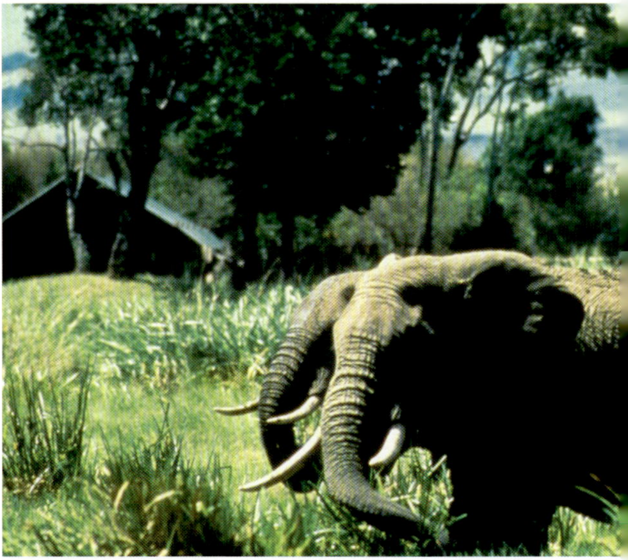

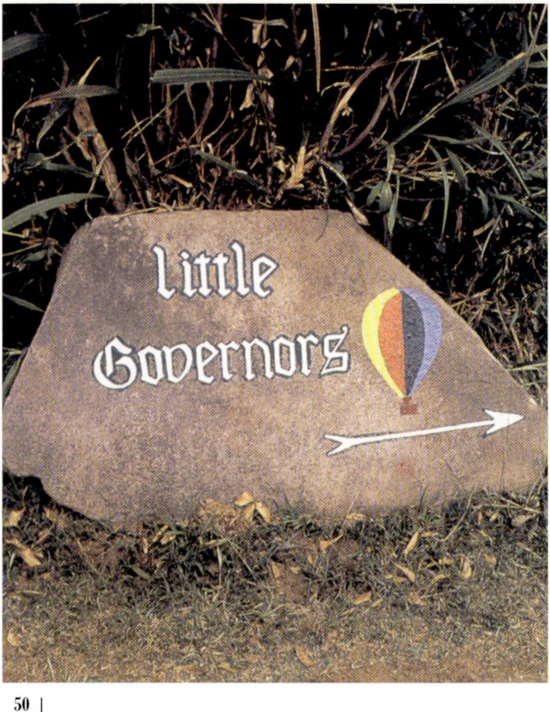
Little
Governors

Left: Elephant investigates tourist camp in the Maasai Mara.

Opposite below: Sign marks one of the Mara's better known luxury camps.

Below: Roosting bird of prey settles for the cool night as the sun sinks over the untamed wilderness of the Maasai Mara.

51

Mara balanites tree silhouetted against the golden glow of fast disappearing day.

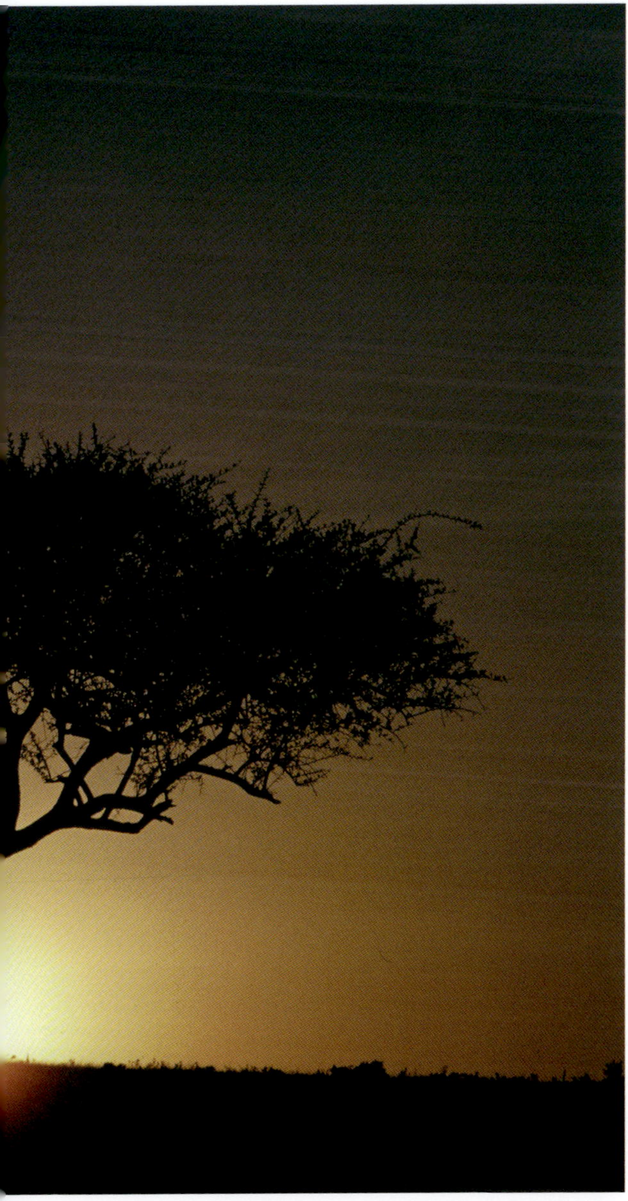

The Mara Country

The Mara knows no seasons – just wet or dry months – yet constantly changes as the year runs its course. Early in the year it is usually dry, with the grasslands often burnt and cropped short. However, there is still a tinge of green from the rains that fell at the back end of the previous year. During April the clouds build up, heralding the onset of the long rains. Folklore has it that when the acacia start to flower rain is near, and the more profuse the flowering the heavier the rain, but it is not always so. The rain brings on the grass, which soon grows tall and ripples in the breeze like water on a lake that is ruffled by the wind.

Rain, when it falls, can be awesome in its fury and volume. Driven by stormy winds it slants down in stinging sheets. Soon the streams fill and with a crescendo of noise the torrent drives stones, dead wood and the debris of nature with it, gouging soil from the banks. Roads and tracks become rivers; the animals stand stoically with backs hunched against the rain, tails between their legs, waiting for the end of the onslaught. The elephants alone seem unmoved. They often come out in the open during heavy rain and carry on feeding.

Now, with grazing and water plentiful, the game disperses and life is harder for the predators. They have to work hard to bring down prey, and soon the ribs on the older lions will show. But better times are near. Around mid-July the land's dominant colour turns from deep green to sandy yellow and, heralded by a noticeable build up of the number of zebra, the mass of wildebeest begin the steady trek from the Serengeti to the Mara. All grass is soon flattened by thousands of sharp hooves, and the rest grazed down.

As the first rush of the incoming migration settles down, the herds spread throughout the Mara and the predators find life much easier. It is often feast and famine for them. Now is the time to feast. Lions kill from habit and because food is readily available. It is not uncommon to come across a pride

The Mara Country

of lions, their bellies gorged, surrounded by barely touched carcasses. Slaughter on such a grand scale provides rich pickings, of course, for the jackal and hyaena.

The grass recovers quickly but mid-October, when it may be tinder-dry, is often a time for fires. Flames, fanned by strong winds, reach great heights and become quite uncontrollable. The only effective control is to cut firebreaks and burn back against the fire – an expensive exercise in manpower and machinery. All too often, a capricious wind turns the flames in the wrong direction frustrating the toiling fire fighters.

In November, there should be enough rain to bring on a new flush of grass, to give the bush and trees heart to put forth new growth, and to top up the streams and surface pans. The yellow and russet plains show green and the land is again one of plenty. It is all part of the Mara pattern, ever changing, with something fresh each day – a new target for the camera lens, a new insight to animal behaviour. No Mara year is ever quite the same.

Lion Cub

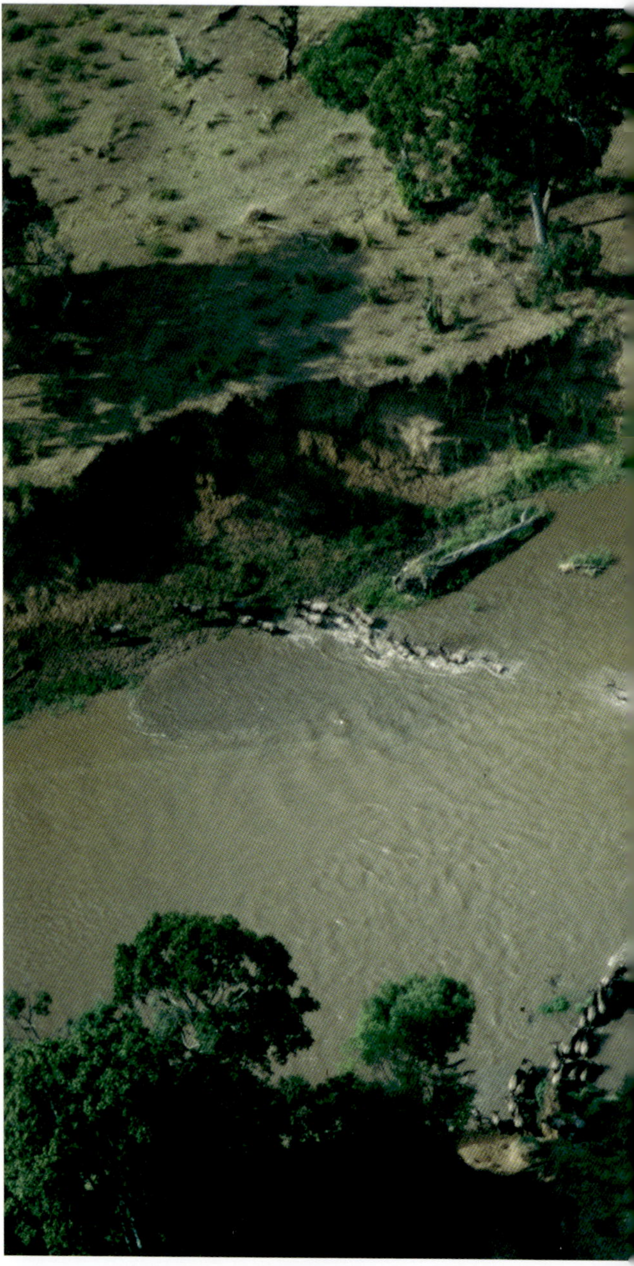

Left: Wildebeest cross the Mara River in a single file during the annual migration.

Above: Up to a million wildebeest ford the Mara River.

Right: When the Mara River is in spate thousands of wildebeest drown or are swept downstream – prey for the river's voracious crocodiles.

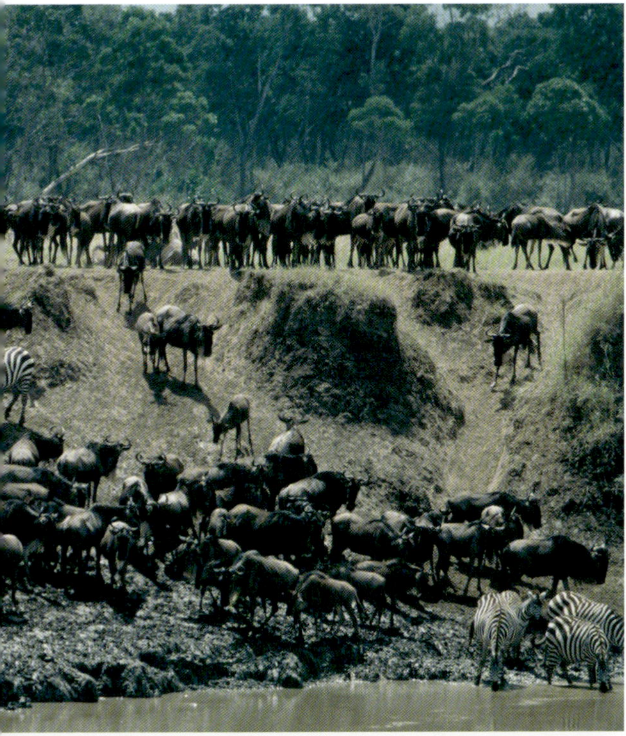

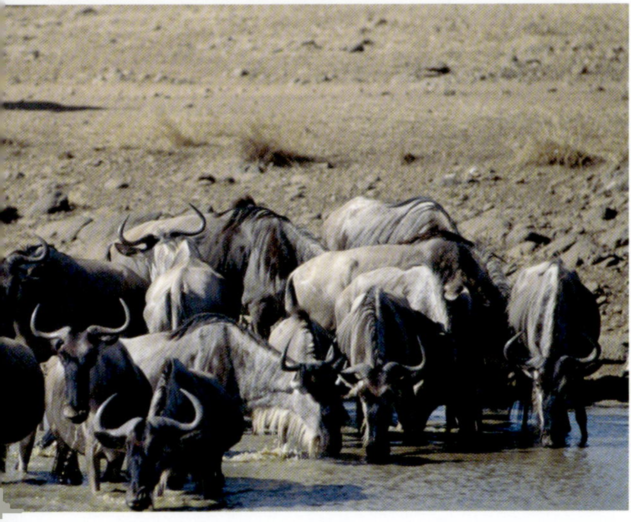

5. The grazers and the browsers

The annual wildebeest migration is one of nature's greatest spectacles and the Maasai Mara plays host to it for four or so months each year. Dr. Bernhard Grzimek first drew public attention to the fact that the Serengeti wildebeest migrated in a definite pattern, in *Serengeti Shall Not Die* published in 1959. By marking large numbers of animals he and his son Michael, who was killed tragically in an aircraft accident during their joint research, were able to track their movements over many months.

The wildebeest's year starts in January on the south-east Serengeti, where the cows give birth. Within a few weeks hundreds of thousands of calves are born on the close-cropped plains. As they emerge into an unwelcoming world, thousands die – snapped up by hyaena and jackal. Though young wildebeest can stand within five minutes of birth and soon run as fast as an adult, the mortality at the most vulnerable time – as the calf emerges from its foetal sac – is quite horrifying to the casual observer.

Soon, the plains grass is cropped to its roots. Water dries up, and the wildebeest move, generally westerly and veering north, in search of new grazing and water. Eventually their continued movement brings them to the Mara, the best-watered part of the ecosystem. Rutting takes place during the northward drift. On their arrival in the Mara the grass is long, but soon gets trampled by the sheer weight of numbers. Residual moisture keeps it growing, and the great mass of wildebeest disperses to cover the entire Mara reserve and (much of the surrounding area) the group ranches to the north and east. As the land dries and the grass dies, the animals regroup and form distinct columns and start wending their way eastwards and southwards.

Their journey takes them over the Mara River, which they traverse using several traditional crossings. It is a remarkable sight as several hundred, and even thousands of animals slither, cautiously at first, down the steep incline to the

The grazers and the browsers

water's edge, the pace of the leaders quickening as pressure builds up from those behind. Amid a cacophony of grunting sounds, one bold wildebeest usually sets the ball rolling with a sudden plunge into the water, accompanied by a wall of spray as it lunges toward the far bank. In the frenzied charge that follows, many perish – trampled underfoot to drown in the muddy waters. In years when the river is low and slow-flowing, the crossings are accomplished without much difficulty. At other times, when the river is full and fast-flowing, the mortality rate is high.

Though an antelope, the wildebeest displays little grace. It is really an absurd-looking animal, with large forequarters sloping to a weak behind, the body supported on spindly legs. They run with a jerky, stiff-legged gait and, for no apparent reason, dart from side to side and kick their hind legs in the air. Yet these clowns of the plains are one of nature's most astonishing success stories, their numbers having risen four to fivefold in 30 years.

The majority of wildebeest that pass through the Mara are migratory, but there is a resident population of several thousand. They stay mainly on the Loita Plains, but form a migration of their own as the rains fall, heading back to the Musiara area to the west of the game reserve. As the main body of migrants return south, they drift back to their usual area on the Loita Plains. It would be interesting to know how many join the Serengeti migration and how many stay behind.

The wildebeest migration is accompanied by about a quarter of a million Burchell's zebra and possibly half a million Thomson's gazelle. The zebra arrive first, their grazing pattern helping the wildebeest. The zebra eat the long woody grass stems, which the wildebeest do not favour. This is another aspect of the grazing succession that helps to maintain the Mara's abundance and diversity of animal species.

Above: **Rutting wildebeest joust and stampede in the dusty frenzy of the migration.**

Opposite top: **Constant attendants of the wildebeest, thousands of zebra also make the annual migration from the deep south of the Serengeti to the Maasai Mara and the Mara River.**

Right: **Wildebeest pause on the migration for a welcome drink.**

63

The grazers and the browsers

Zebra stripes are like fingerprints, unique to the individual. The zebra is not a herd animal, but stays in family groups headed by a dominant stallion. In the Mara most females give birth between January and March. The foals, which can stand within an hour, begin to graze about 10 days after birth. The zebra's call, a high-pitched yelp somewhere between a dog's bark and a donkey's bray, is a familiar sound on the plains for most of the year. At mating time there is considerable activity as young stallions are attracted to the young females in oestrus. When the dominant stallion tries to fight the others off some spectacular battles take place. The males rear at each other, forelegs flailing and teeth bared, before turning to deliver scything kicks. As the females stay in oestrus for a week, the family stallion has his work cut out to keep his favoured females under control. He is not always successful. Many mares are abducted and served by several young stallions. As the mares become older their oestrus postures are less pronounced and attract less attention, and they tend to submit to the dominant stallion.

Thomson's gazelle, the Tommy, named after the explorer Joseph Thomson, is a familiar species and a third component of the annual migration. While a great number of Thomson's are resident, probably half a million are migrants. It is unmistakable in appearance, with a sandy fawn back, a rufous tinge, a black stripe running along the flanks, white belly and white rump, and a stubby black tail that is in constant motion. The strongly ringed horns rise from the skull to bend back in a gentle curve, becoming vertical at the tips, which are smooth.

The Thomson's gazelle is sometimes confused with the Grant's, though it shouldn't be. The Grant's is named after James Grant who accompanied Speke on his journey to discover the source of the Nile. It is larger, lighter coloured and the black stripe along the flank is absent in the adults. It

The grazers and the browsers

has a chestnut stripe down the face and a dark nose spot. The horns are lyre-shaped, and heavily ringed. A sub-species of Grant's gazelle, Robert's, is common in the Mara. The horns are less lyrate, and diverge widely at a point about one-third of their length from the base, so that the tips are far apart with a backward twist at the extremities.

Both species are common throughout the Mara, with the Tommy principally a grazer and the Grant's more a browser. The Tommy has a gestation period of five months and may breed twice a year. Though they may give birth at any time of the year, the greater numbers of fawn arrive between January and July. The females often drop the newborn fawns and stroll away apparently unconcerned, giving the impression they have abandoned their young. This is a ploy to deter predators, for a young Tommy is easy prey for any carnivore and avian raptor. For the first week or two the fawn lies close among the grass tussocks. The female suckles several times a day but spends most of her time grazing quietly, some distance from the youngster. Young Thomson's gazelle often adopt a peculiar stiff-legged trot, called stotting, when alarmed or in play.

The largest antelope, the eland, is common in the Mara. A stately animal – pale fawn or tawny in colour, becoming lighter underneath, with a variable number of vertical stripes on the body – it is shy and difficult to approach. In both sexes, the smooth horns have a screw-like spiral in the basal half. The adult bull has a blackish tuft of bushy hair on the forehead with a large dewlap hanging from the throat. Eland are normally found in parties of between a dozen and 20, though they may combine to form larger groups of up to one hundred. Old bulls are often solitary. Both browsers and grazers, they can go long periods without water. Though large, measuring some two metres at the shoulder and weighing up to 1,000 kilos, the eland is extraordinarily docile. Maasai used to capture young eland bulls and run

Above: Magnificent lyrate horns of the Impala, loveliest of all antelope.

Opposite top: From the moment of birth young Thomson's gazelle learn to freeze in a prone position to avoid alerting predators.

Opposite: Waterbuck, one of the many species of antelope and plains game that crowd the golden grasslands of the Maasai Mara.

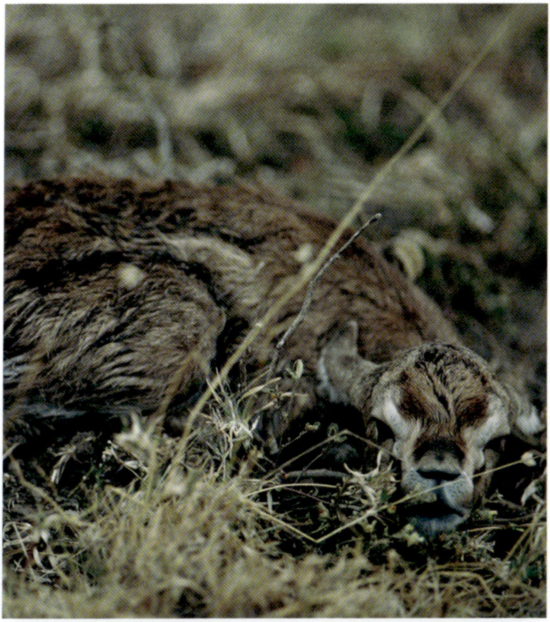

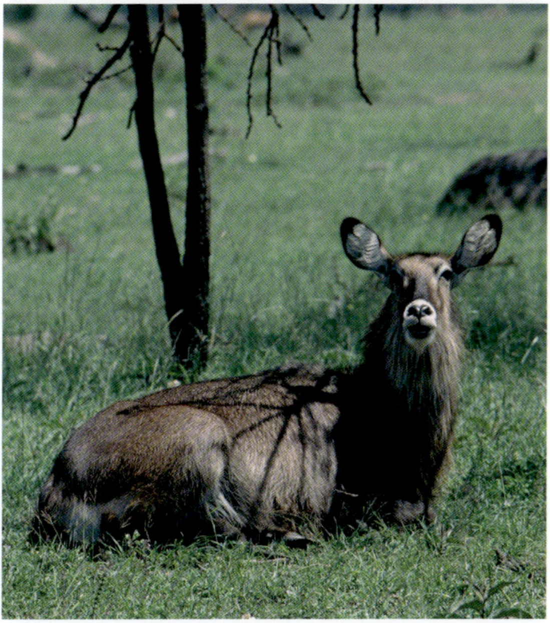

The grazers and the browsers

them with the domestic herd to improve the quality of meat and milk. The males are more sedentary than the females, and the large groups contain one dominant bull with a few younger males, the greater number being females with calves of varying ages. Despite generations of exposure to vehicles and intensive tourism, the Mara eland have lost none of their inherent wariness, and start moving in their extended, swinging trot long before they are in camera range.

Two hartebeests – the Topi and Coke's hartebeest, or Kongoni, are members of the ungainly wildebeest clan. They are neither beautiful nor graceful. The topi, related to the tiang of Sudan and tsessebe of Southern Africa, are the better looking with blue-black thighs and yellow stockings. A large group with the sun shining on their iridescent backs makes a pretty sight. The males are territorial, regularly trampling and marking their stamping grounds, and though herds normally run at around 20 to 40 animals, at certain times of the year concentrations reach as many as a thousand animals. Hartebeest and topi males frequently stand on an ant-hill or other vantage point. They may look half-asleep and not particularly alert but, in fact, keep a very close look out. Impending danger is acknowledged by a snort and foot stamping, before flight in an odd, rocking horse-like canter.

There is no question that one of the most beautiful and graceful of all antelope is the impala, and happily the Mara has an abundance of these delightful creatures. The lyrate horns are present only in the male, but both sexes share the rich chestnut coat and large eyes. Impala are found in all the varied Mara habitats, in large herds composed of a herd male and a variable number of females. It is believed the males are territorial. When females enter a territory a strong male will gather as many as he can into a breeding herd. Vigorous males claim as many as 50 females, but spend much of their time circling them to cut off deserters and win a few more. Not far away will be groups of males,

The grazers and the browsers

some of them youngsters evicted by the herd male, others older males which keep an eye open for a straggling female to start their own herd. After banishment from the main herd, young males are vulnerable to predators and there are fewer males than females.

It is a taxing job holding a bunch of female impala together and, inevitably, the time comes when the herd male is challenged. Impala males are known to fight to the death, usually wrestling with horns locked, each trying to throw the other off balance. The weaker male, quite often the herd male who is in poorer condition than his challenger, will give way when he has had enough and wander off to join one of the bachelor herds and await another day. Intensely alert, a high-pitched, sneezy snort of alarm is often the signal for rapid flight in a series of graceful leaps.

The impala is both browser and grazer, and makes use of a variety of plant species. When a female gives birth she usually leaves the herd and secludes herself and her fawn in a patch of bush, remaining there for a few days before rejoining the herd, where the fawn becomes the centre of considerable interest.

The largest grazer is the hippo. In daylight it spends most of its time immersed in the Mara River or pools that sustain its bulk. At night the hippo – probably the Behemoth of the Bible – leaves the water to seek grass and other vegetation. Some places along the river show deep ruts, caused by regular passage of the hippo as they walk inland in search of food. The three-metre-long, non-ruminating stomach needs a great deal of herbage to satisfy it and hippo cause enormous damage to cultivated areas, through feeding and trampling. The hippo is really a huge, unwieldy, specialised pig, with a large barrel-shaped body and a vast swollen muzzle. The teeth were once sought after as ivory for they do not discolour like elephant ivory. Hippo are gregarious, and families are found in large groups.

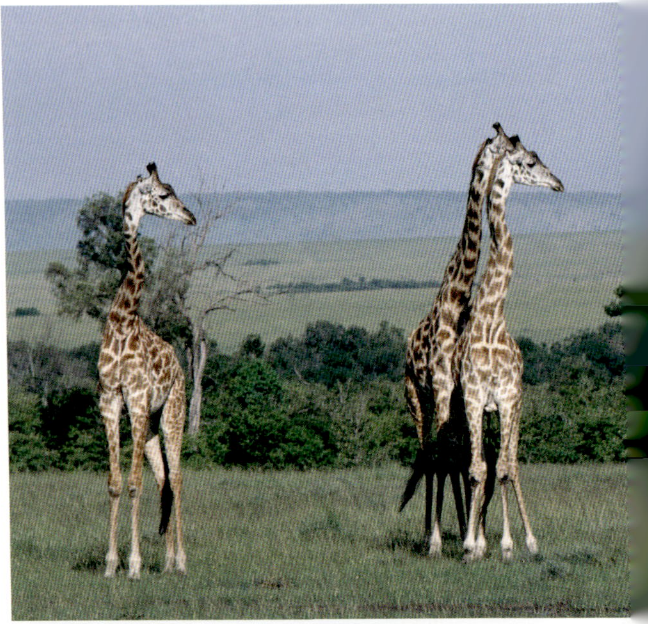

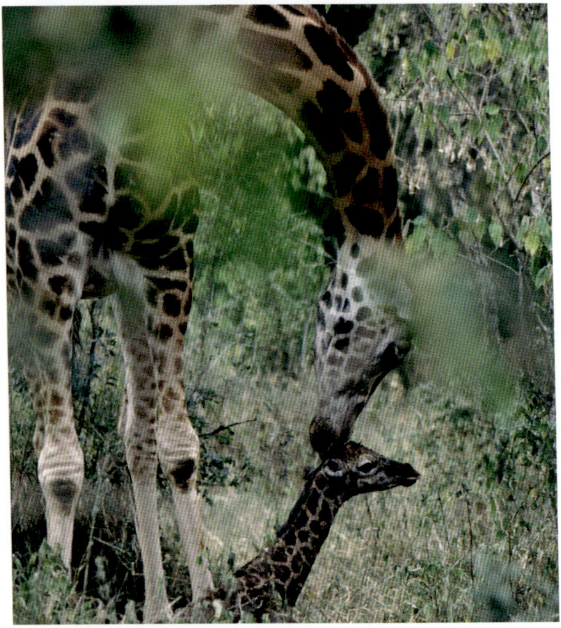

Above: Giraffe – a familiar sight wherever you travel through the Maasai Mara.

Opposite: Mother giraffe welcomes new-born youngster to life in the Mara.

The grazers and the browsers

A single calf is produced after a gestation period of eight months or so. The adult males indulge in fearful, noisy battles that may last days and nights, inflicting dreadful injuries on one another despite their thick skin.

The most obvious Mara browser is the Maasai giraffe, the tallest animal on earth. An adult bull could measure some 12 feet at the shoulder, with another six feet of neck, and weigh about 1,000 kilos. They may be found singly, in small groups, or in herds of as many as 50. Dignified, aloof and with an appearance of gentleness, the giraffe is a much-loved animal, with eyelashes the envy of any film star. The sparring behaviour, known as 'necking', is fascinating. It is performed only by males and is, in fact, a form of fighting. Two males stand shoulder to shoulder and, in apparent slow motion, appear to wrap their long necks around each other. This may go on for a long time, with a series of pauses as if the giraffe are stopping to think about things. As the battle becomes more intense they swing their heads at each other with considerable force, aiming at the neck and body – a shrewd blow could break a neck.

One curious feature of the giraffe's social organisation is the nursery. A group of young giraffe may be left in the care of one or two females, even occasionally unattended. The nursery is usually on high ground to which the mothers return periodically. The reason for this has not been satisfactorily explained. Researchers have found a high mortality rate for calves up to three months old, and relatively few survive beyond a year, most taken by predators.

It is quite a performance when giraffe drink. With considerable loss of dignity they spread their legs and bend their knees to get their long neck down to water. They drink briefly then jerk their heads up and snap their legs together before cautiously looking for danger. This ungainly performance is repeated several times before their thirst is satisfied. The giraffe's neck contains an intricate system of

The grazers and the browsers

valves with extremely elastic and absorbent blood vessels that prevent the blood flowing too quickly from the brain.

At such times the giraffe is vulnerable to predators. Its size and speed makes the adult giraffe generally safe from predators, but lions have been known to kill them.

There is a host of smaller herbivores in the Mara. The handsome bushbuck, with its dark rufous back and single spiral horns, is a forest-dweller and more likely to be seen in the early morning or evening. The reedbuck, sandy coloured with stubby horns that extend forward at the tip, is usually seen singly or in pairs along gullies and riverbanks. The tiny dik dik, standing a mere 40 centimetres at the shoulder, is often seen in pairs in the drier country. The klipspringer, found in rocky places, stands on the tips of its hooves, which are cylindrical and adapted to clinging to rock. They take some spotting as their light sandy coat blends so well with their surroundings. They are normally seen in pairs or singly.

There about 25 species of grazers and browsers in the Maasai Mara, some small and rarely seen, others large and obvious. They are all part of the unique and enthralling mix that is the Mara – a mix that brings so many people back time and again to savour the experience.

6. The big shots – Elephant, Buffalo and Rhino

Next to man no other mammal has so profound an influence upon its habitat, or other species that share it, as does the elephant. It is the agent of change in many African ecosystems. Often stark scientific fact dispels any aura of romance or mysticism about an animal but not in the case of the elephant. Many human qualities have been ascribed to it – sagacity, memory, longevity, emotion, and even a sense of humour. Myths and legends surround it in abundance and testify to mankind's fascination with the elephant down the centuries.

Today its plight commands great attention beyond the confines of Africa. Perhaps the parallels between human and elephant are partly responsible for the heightened interest. Certainly its bulky majesty cannot be ignored in any conservation context. Like us, elephant are born into families that show interest and concern for its members. The families live in close contact with their relatives, sharing the same ranges. A mother's ties with her young do not disappear with the arrival of new offspring, but continue as long-lasting bonds. There are many recorded cases of senile matriarchs kept in tow by their family unit after they have lost their senses.

The females form closely-related units that live in close and frequent contact with other groups. It is in the female sector of elephant activity that mankind finds many parallels. As the young males reach puberty they are driven away from the family herd by senior females. The bulls become satellites of the family unit and hang around the fringes. Among similarly displaced age-mates the young male develops friendships and loose bonds. Between the ages of 20 and 25 growth accelerates. The now adult male starts to come into *musth*, a phenomenon only recently described in the African elephant and characterised by a radical change in hormone balances. Levels of the male hormone, testosterone, soar by upto four times and the temporal glands start to discharge. There is a constant dribble of urine from the penis.

The big shots – Elephant, Buffalo and Rhino

The onset of *musth* changes the normally placid male into an irritable creature, given a wide berth by other males. The musth bull will move out of its normal range to look for females in oestrus. After several weeks the high testosterone levels drop, the bull resumes his composure and returns to his normal range until, months later, the next *musth* begins. The facts concerning *musth* in the African elephant – it is well known in the Indian elephant – come from two independent sources. Cynthia Moss and Joyce Poole, both zoologists, observed elephants in the Amboseli over a long period, and another zoologist, Anthony Hall-Martin, worked in the Addo and Kruger National Parks in South Africa.

Elephant have a prodigious ability to alter their surroundings. In Uganda's Murchison Falls National Park they eliminated the tall forest, with all its animal and plant species, and brought about its replacement with grassland. This effect has been seen in many of Africa's parks. Today there are between 1,000 and 2,000 elephants in the Maasai Mara depending on migrations. The elephants have largely been responsible for opening up the land. This form of gardening may be beneficial, but as elephant ranges are more restricted and food must be found from more limited areas, fears grow that the authorities may be forced to control, in some way, the increase in the elephant population at a time when, ironically, vast sums of money are being raised for its preservation.

Not to be outdone the African or Southern Buffalo, is a force to reckon with and a giant in its own right. Few animals are more inflicted with such a reputation for ferocity and ill-temper than the buffalo. There are many hunters' stories of men badly injured or killed by a wounded buffalo. Fear and instinctive defence often prompt an animal to aggression, and a disturbed buffalo is no exception. A lone male lying up in thick bush is extremely dangerous and unpredictable when disturbed.

Giraffe at sundown.

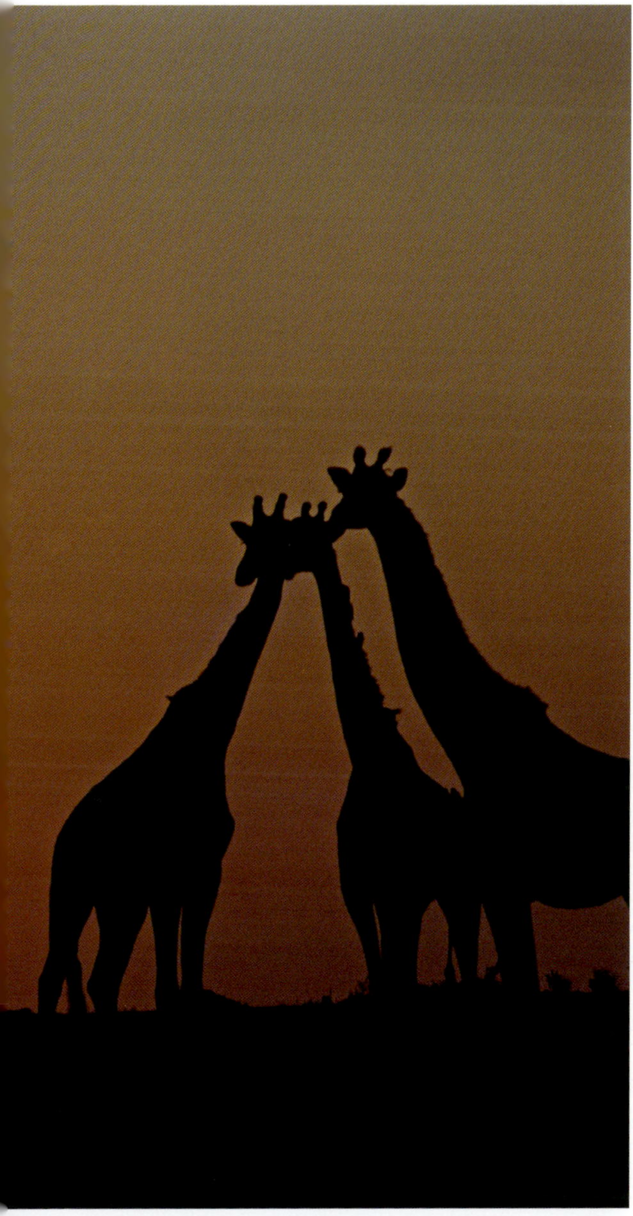

The big shots – Elephant, Buffalo and Rhino

Normally, however, buffalo are placid, and large herds, several hundred strong, may be seen all over the Mara. Groups of elderly males, their breeding days done, stay together for long periods and, being slow in reaction and stiff in the legs, are slowly picked off by lions. Man has been the buffalo's most destructive foe, while their only natural enemy is the lion which, in addition to picking off the elderly bachelors, hang round the fringes of a herd hoping to isolate a calf or young heifer. There are hazards for the lion, though. It is not unusual for a group of young bulls, when scenting lion, to bunch together and charge the predators and scatter them into deep bush. There are many reports of lion being killed by buffalo in one-to-one combat. Big bulls have a mighty kick and often inflict severe damage with their heavy horns mounted on their powerful necks.

Then there are the rhino. In 1971 there were probably 120 black rhinoceros in the Maasai Mara. By 1984 there were a mere 18. The appalling decline was not confined to just the Mara. Throughout Africa vast numbers of rhino were butchered to satisfy a market greedy for horn. Only in the late 1980s was the decline halted in the Mara, and the good news in 1993 was that it was reversed and numbers were rising. Today there are about 30, almost all east of the Maasai River. Since 1984 a system of daily surveillance, involving a vehicle and a trained crew, has been in operation. Twice each day the rhino are observed, their well-being checked, their movements plotted and any signs of illegal activity investigated.

It has been a natural restocking, for no alien rhino have been translocated from elsewhere. The result is that the present population is predominantly young, with an even balance between males and females. Surveillance has yielded considerable knowledge of rhino behaviour, diet and movement. Each Mara rhino is named and, with readily recognisable characteristics, is easily identified by a skilled observer.

The big shots – Elephant, Buffalo and Rhino

The black rhino has three toes on both fore and hind legs, and its spoor is easily recognised. It is principally a browser, and uses its triangular prehensile upper lip to strip shrubs and bushes of the twigs and leaves on which it feeds. It tends to be solitary, but not exclusively so. When more than one is seen it is usually a cow and her calf, or a mating pair.

Sometimes two males link up and stay together for a while. Occasionally several animals group together for short periods. These are often loose family groups, a cow with a calf at foot plus an earlier calf and possibly two males with an interest in mating with the adult female. One calf is born after a gestation of between 16 to 18 months, although shorter periods have been recorded. The Mara matriarchs, the old cows that survived the bleak years of massive poaching, now produce a calf every two years.

The rhino horn, so sought after for medicines and decorated dagger handles, in fact is a closely compressed mass of agglutinated hair and keratin, with no connection to the skull. It is possible for a rhino to wrench off its horn, merely leaving a skin wound. It grows again, and in areas where rhino have had their horns sawn off to discourage poachers, the rate of growth has been such that within two or three years the horn is back to roughly its former length.

Africa's other rhino species, the white rhino, has never, so far as is known, occurred naturally in the Mara. There was once a northern variety, which disappeared long ago and which was found in Uganda, parts of Central Africa, the Sudan and possibly western Kenya. Once seriously endangered, the southern White rhinoceros, *Ceratotherium simum* is found in southern Africa and, being of a more equable temperament, has accepted a more confined, ranch-type way of life quite happily. It is this that led to its recovery from the brink of extinction to today's healthy numbers.

To call it white is a misnomer, for it is usually a uniform dirty grey. Like the elephant, both species of rhino take on

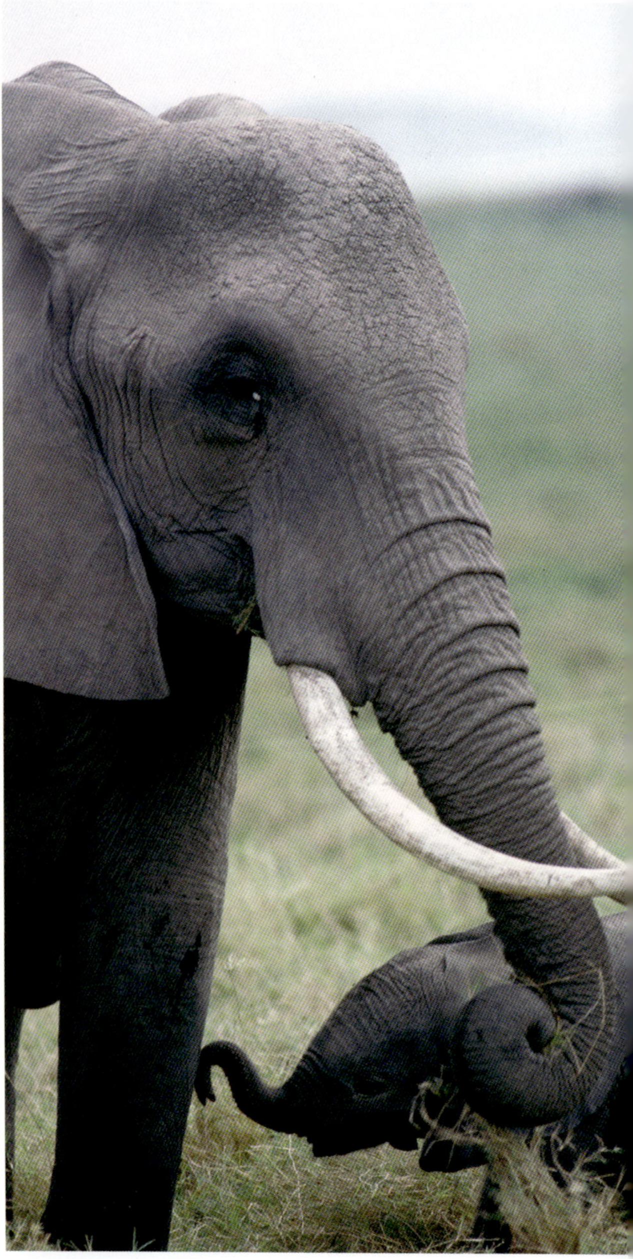

Left: Mother elephant guides young calf.

Elephant fords the Mara River.

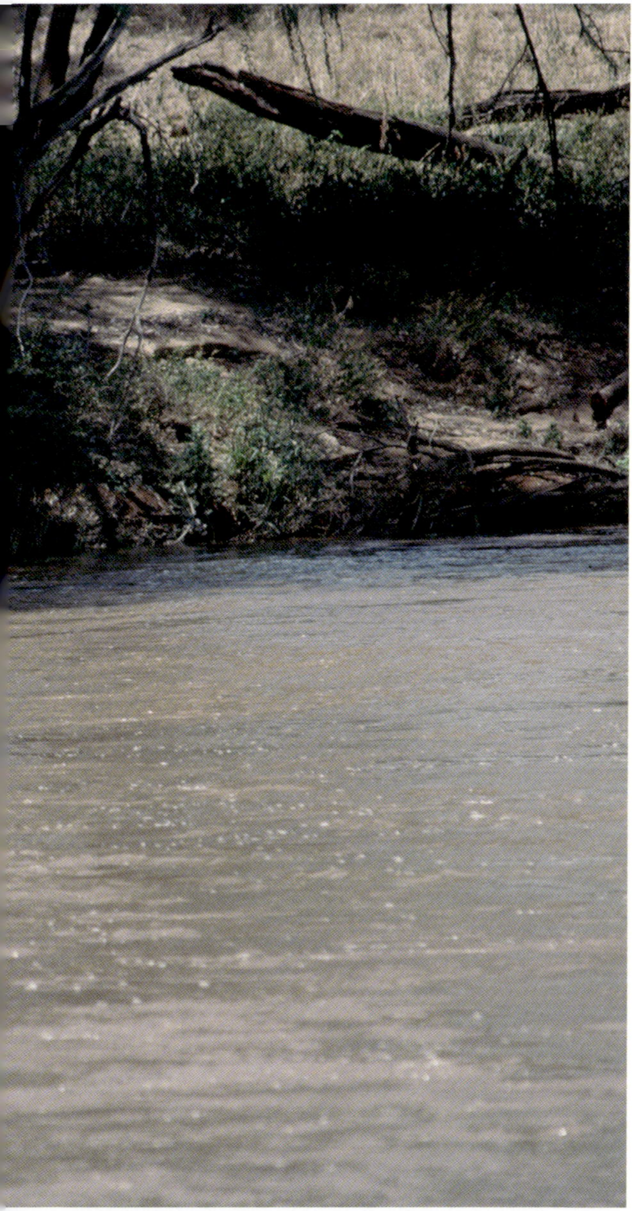

The big shots – Elephant, Buffalo and Rhino

the colour of the earth they wallow or roll in. It is popularly assumed the white rhino was given its name because of its wide, or square-lipped mouth, from the Afrikaans word 'wyt', meaning wide. (The black rhino could be described as the 'hook-lipped' rhino, from its prehensile, triangular shaped upper lip). Another version is that the rhino appeared white in the sunlight after wallowing. Whatever the name source, it is a very different animal from the Mara's black rhino.

An essential difference is that it is a grazer, preferring open grass plains to thick bush. It is also a more placid animal and has none of its congener's reputation for unprovoked aggression and uncertain temper. These traits have helped it to become an animal with a fairly secure future. It adapts well to a managed existence, and game ranches in southern Africa have found no difficulty in rearing the white rhino. Now there is a regular market in the species. Animals are bought and sold for stocking new ranches, and for introducing different blood lines to the established older populations.

All white rhino in Kenya are either imported or descended from imported stock. The remarkable Solio Ranch in Laikipia, north of Nairobi, has bred the largest population in Kenya and has supplied animals for stocking the Nakuru National Park, among others.

Recently, white rhino were imported to Ol Choro – Oirouwa ranch to the north of the National Reserve. Originally two were translocated. Presently the two animals which remain are kept in a compound near Kileleoni, close to the location of Mara Safari Club. It will be of considerable interest to watch the progress of these alien animals in an alien environment and in an area that has seen no genuine Mara black rhino for several years. This means there will be no conflict of interest. They readily accept herding and being escorted, feed in the open, are more visible and

The big shots – Elephant, Buffalo and Rhino

more approachable by visitors than the shyer black variety. Should this first cautious venture be a success then perhaps the Mara may look forward to the permanent settlement of a new immigrant species – compensation enough, perhaps, for the disappearance of the splendid roan antelope.

The black rhino has an ill-deserved reputation for stupidity and aggressiveness. While they have good hearing and sense of smell, their eyesight is poor. Being inquisitive they trot briskly to investigate an unknown scent. As curiosity mounts they may increase speed leading people to believe they are being charged. Certainly hunters, and others, have perished in the path of charging rhino. As rhino generally stick to a regular path, and weigh a ton or more, a fragile human stands little chance of surviving the impact. The rhino reacts quickly to alarm. When their accompanying tick birds fly off with a panic chattering, the rhino leaps to its feet, swings its massive head from side to side trying to pick up scent and, while lumbering in the direction from which it senses danger, it emits a series of snorts. Thus it has earned its name as an irritable, rather dumb curmudgeon and best avoided. The majority of the Mara rhino are placid and easy going, though some are shy and difficult to find. Others spend much of their time in the open and are easily approachable.

There is one behavioural feature of interest – its way of depositing dung. The rhino habitually drops its dung at certain points, used regularly. After defecating it scrapes its hind legs through the deposit, and may sometimes rootle it about with its horn. Other rhinos may use the same dung heap, which may become a sizeable pile in the course of time. Scientists still haven't worked out the reason for this behaviour. The rhino is not territorial, in that it does not defend its home patch. It does have a range beyond which it rarely wanders, and which it seems content to share with others. Perhaps the dung scraping is a method

The big shots – Elephant, Buffalo and Rhino

of communication, to let others know who is passing through, and doing what.

Even the kindest person could not call a rhino beautiful and it has few friends. It is also easy to kill and its plight should concern us all. At least for the moment, the Maasai Mara gives hope that its steadily rising population will be left in peace. John Goddard, the young Canadian biologist who studied the Ngorongoro rhino in the 1960s, and to whom we owe so much knowledge of the black rhinoceros, once said in a television documentary: "(The rhino) is a short-sighted, harmless old beast that deserves, I think, the greatest degree of sympathy that you can give it".

Lion

Black rhino enjoys a wallow in a Mara mudhole.

Female cheetah with cubs.

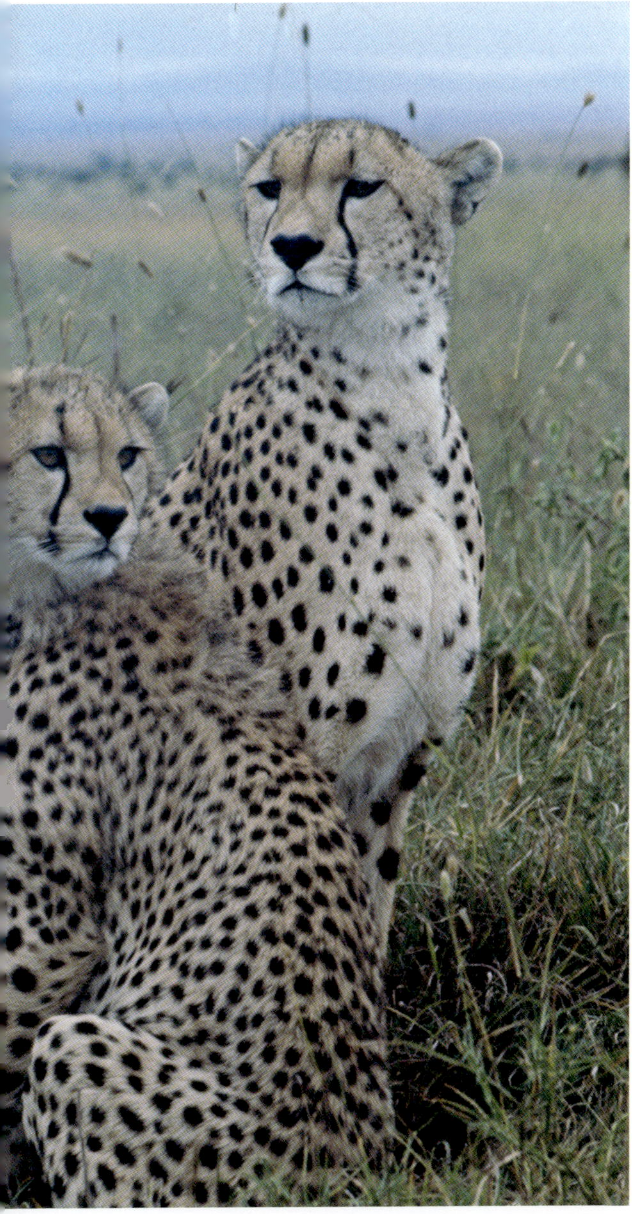

7. The Hunters – the Big Cats

The lion is the one animal every visitor to the Mara wants to see, and disappointment is rare indeed. The Maasai respect the lion – for its sagacity, strength, and nobility, and no other animal provokes a greater reaction. To kill a lion in daylight was considered a great honour and to take part in the hunt a privilege. The mane was prized as a headdress for a moran, and could only be worn by the moran who had either killed the lion or made the first spear thrust. Today these are rarely seen, and the few that remain are prized as family heirlooms.

Lion have long played a role in mythology. In ancient Egypt the town of Leontopolis was named after a cult of lion worshippers. The Greek goddess Cybele was drawn in a chariot harnessed to two lions. The Romans used them as executioners and sacrifices. In medieval Europe, physicians claimed the fat cured swollen glands, carbuncles and growths, and the dried and powdered blood, cancer.

Lion have been studied extensively, most notably by American zoologist George Schaller in the Serengeti. They are perhaps the best understood of the big cats. The basis of lion society is the resident pride – founded on a lioness or lionesses – which occupies the same territory for long periods, maybe several generations. Female offspring provide continuity and are the permanent members of the group. Many Mara prides were founded many generations ago and have occupied the same areas for decades.

The pride has its adult males, though they tend to be transient. They attain hierarchical positions by evicting their predecessors, often after a series of vicious and bloody battles. Young males leave the pride under pressure from the senior male as they approach the adult stage, usually between their second and fourth years. They will either wander alone for a time or link with one or two others of the same age. When fully mature they may establish themselves within a pride by ousting a resident male.

The Hunters – the Big Cats

They then settle among the pride until they, in turn, are ousted. When a new male takes over a pride he often kills the cubs sired by his predecessor. This induces the rapid onset of oestrus in the females, and allows the new lord and master to father his own progeny.

The size of a pride is probably governed by available food. Food is usually abundant in the Mara, where prides may number as many as 40 animals – males, females and cubs of varying ages. When numbers become too great for the available food, young lionesses may become as nomadic as the males. The lion does not always live up to its reputation as a hunter. It is an inveterate scavenger and ever on the lookout for other predators' kills. Whenever possible, it will drive away the legitimate owner and claim the kill.

When they do hunt, lion will kill whatever is easiest and most readily available. The hunt, usually initiated by the females, happens more often in the early morning or late evening though prey may be pursued at any time of day. The technique is one of stealth, to stalk cautiously to within a few paces of the victim, make a fast rush and pull it down, killing either by a bite through the neck or by clamping on the muzzle with powerful jaws until it suffocates. When several females take part in a hunt, it is conducted almost like a military operation, with diversions, pincer movements and a final assault carried out with precision. There is no apparent communication between the animals, yet there seems to be perfect understanding; but when one makes a mistake, or is too hasty in her approach and the prey escapes, her companions' looks of disgust are undisguised.

When prey is finally pulled down there is a remarkable lack of social decorum. The biggest and strongest take what they want, and the smaller and weaker make do with what they can snatch. The feeding is accompanied by a fearful growling and snarling, and the scavengers – the jackals and

Above: A Mara lion greets its inquisitive young progeny.

Right: Mara lioness and cubs.

Left: Mara lioness.

Below: Lioness takes up a vantage point on a knoll to scout for prey.

The Hunters – the Big Cats

vultures – lurk on the fringes in the hope of picking up the leftovers. Between them and the hyaena, within a few hours, there will be few visible signs of the feast.

Gestation is between three and four months and the young are born in litters of up to nine, though they usually number between two and four. Blind until about their 14th day they remain hidden for some eight weeks, when they are brought out to meet the rest of the pride. It is a remarkable sight to watch the emergence of the tiny cubs, carried in the mother's mouth, to be deposited among the older females who take an immediate maternal interest in the new arrivals.

The lion's roar is a familiar Mara sound, usually at night. It is both a challenge and a declaration of territorial possession. It is also a proclamation of presence, made to avoid direct confrontation. Nomadic lions normally move away when they hear another's roar.

Some Mara males develop fine manes, many quite black. There are few more splendid sights than a pair of black-maned lions, lying or sitting on their haunches on an anthill or other promontory, a gentle breeze ruffling their magnificent manes – kings, indeed, of all they survey. The tip of the lion's tail is black, too, and conceals a claw which, legend would have us believe, he uses to lash himself into a fury when need be. The cubs have spots that last well into adulthood.

Lion have always been a feature of the Mara, one of the few places where one can be fairly sure of meeting black-maned males. They have adapted well to the demands of visitors and over the years have become not just accustomed to vehicles but contemptuous of those that approach too closely and intrude on their lives. It is estimated that there are some 400-500 lions in the Mara area. Recent research suggests that lions remain "resident" rather than following the migrations as was once thought. As the lion represents power and grandeur, so the leopard stands for beauty and ferocity. It is a shy, nocturnal animal and not often seen.

The Hunters – the Big Cats

When sighted it rightly evokes admiration for it is a truly beautiful animal. It is the most widespread of the cats and thus varies greatly according to its habitat. However, there is only one species and 'panther' is a synonym for leopard. It is found over much of sub-Saharan Africa, and across the southern part of Asia to southern China.

The Mara leopard is richly coloured. The spots, on the back and flanks, are a series of rings or rosettes, the centres of which are the same yellowish tawny as the rest of the coat. Along the back the spots often meet to form a continuous dark line, but on the head, neck, limbs and tail the spots are usually solid black. The black panthers of Asia seem to be unspotted but underlying spots can be seen on careful inspection. In Kenya melanistic black leopards may be found in high country, the Aberdare range for example, but they are rare.

Being shy and secretive, and with their coats providing perfect camouflage in the dappled light under bush and tree, leopards are hard to spot. Many people who have spent a lifetime in the African wild can count on their fingers the times they have seen a leopard in daylight. They would have been grouped among the most rare animals on the continent, were it not for the fact that their tracks and their liking for carrion give ample evidence of their presence. They come readily to rotting meat and therefore are among the easiest of the cats to trap. One has only to drag a carcass through the bush for a short distance, secure it in the fork of a tree out of reach of scavengers – and a leopard will soon arrive.

Leopard have a wide range of recorded food, from beetles to a full-grown eland bull – an animal thirteen times its own weight. In India, and parts of East Africa, leopards have become habitual man-eaters. A study of leopard dung in Tsavo National Park in Kenya revealed a large proportion of small rodent remains, bird parts and insect fragments. The ability to live off very small creatures explains how leopards can survive inoffensively and unknown among fairly dense human populations.

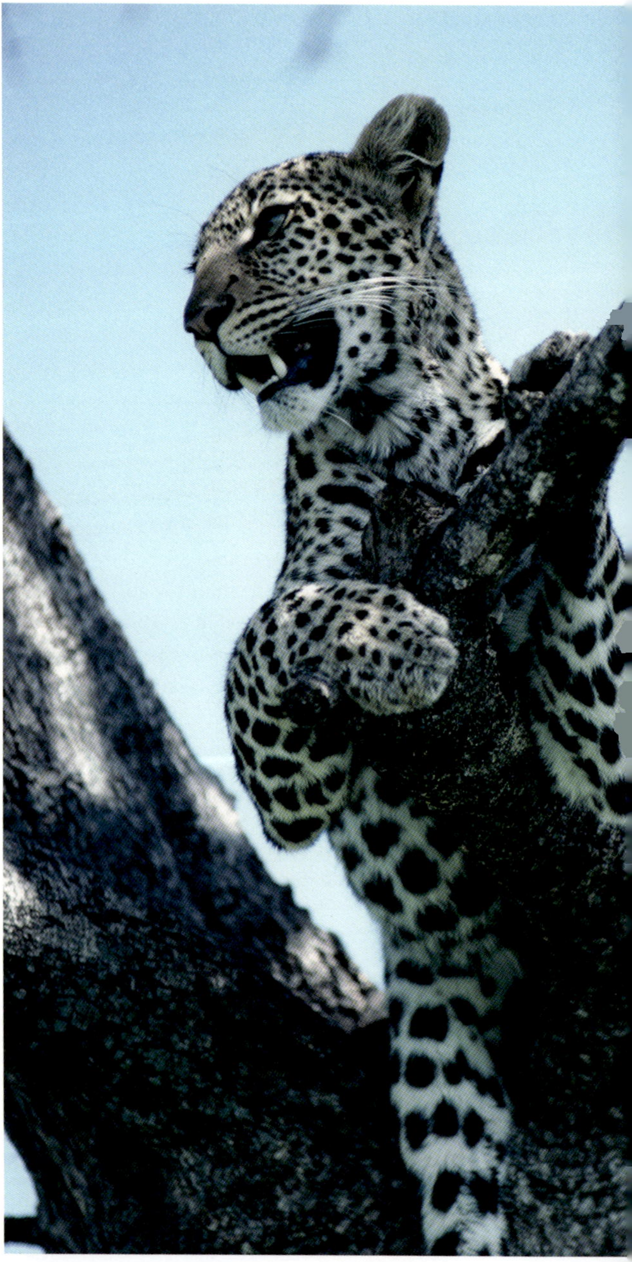

Above: A leopard relaxes on a tree.

Left: Leopard on a tree lair. Maasai Mara is one of the few places on earth where it is possible to see these nocturnal creatures by day.

The Hunters – the Big Cats

Like most cats, leopards are territorial though their ranges are not exclusive and overlap to a degree. Through scent and sound individuals advertise their whereabouts to others and thus avoid contact.

Leopards are skilled climbers and often drop on their unsuspecting quarry from above. Zoologist Jonathan Kingdon describes the method: "... there is a common pattern to the leopard's killing technique, the first action of which consists of a strike with claws extended. This may be a flip, scoop, swat or slamming embrace, the strength and orientation of the movement being graded according to size and location of the prey. This is followed by a bite that is generally directed at the neck or back of the head while the paws embrace the body".

The leopard habitually carries its kill high up a tree, out of reach of all but insects, and wedges it firmly in a fork – to be eaten at leisure. The more putrid it becomes the more palatable to the leopard. The dried skin and bone of an old kill is an indication of a leopard's 'larder' and a promising sign that it is still in the vicinity.

Man has long prized the leopard pelt as fine apparel. In Africa the skins were hallmarks of royalty and prestige. At one time there was a large and expensive fashion market for beautifully tailored leopard coats and jackets in America and Europe. In the mid-1960s tens of thousands of leopard skins left Africa and Asia each year, providing a stark illustration of how abundant these seemingly rare cats were. The trade has all but ceased, following a campaign that was so successful that any fashion-conscious woman today would rather walk the streets of New York or Paris naked than clad in a leopard skin coat.

But the leopard is not every man's favourite animal. It is a ruthless stock-killer and generally detested by the Maasai. It is feared, too, as dangerous when cornered. A wounded leopard will almost certainly charge if its place of

The Hunters – the Big Cats

concealment is approached and can rarely be stopped except by death. It moves fast and its method of attack is usually to scalp its aggressor with its wicked claws.

On the whole the leopard is a silent animal, but it does give utterance to a harsh, grating, grunting cough several times in succession. After each grunt the breath is drawn in and the whole produces a double effect, perhaps best described as the sound of wood being sawn. An angry leopard coughs and growls rather like a similarly ill-disposed lion.

Few sights are more impressive than a leopard stretched along a low fever tree branch, or lying on a rock enjoying the early morning sun. The cubs are born in some kind of deep shelter – a rock cave or even a deep hole in the ground, normally two to four in a litter. In certain areas of the Mara the very fortunate have watched young cubs at play in full daylight. Though man's hand is so often set against it, the leopard is a survivor and likely to be around long after the last lion has been exterminated.

Nothing could be more temperamentally different from the leopard than the cheetah. It has spots and is a large cat, but there the similarity just about ends. It is not a true cat, in fact, having blunt claws (like those of a dog) that can only partially be withdrawn. It is distinguished by its long legs and body, small head and true spots – dotted solidly, unlike the rosettes of the leopard. Long dark lines extend from the inner corners of the eyes to the sides of the upper lip, and are entirely characteristic. Though they are not nearly so common as the leopard they are more frequently seen, and the Mara is one of the best places in the world to find them.

The cheetah's method of hunting is peculiar to the species, and quite unlike that of other cats. It is built for speed, and hunts by stalking close to its prey and then racing after it, bringing it down before seizing it by the throat and suffocating it. Being a sprinter it cannot maintain great pace for long, and if it has not caught its victim within 100 metres

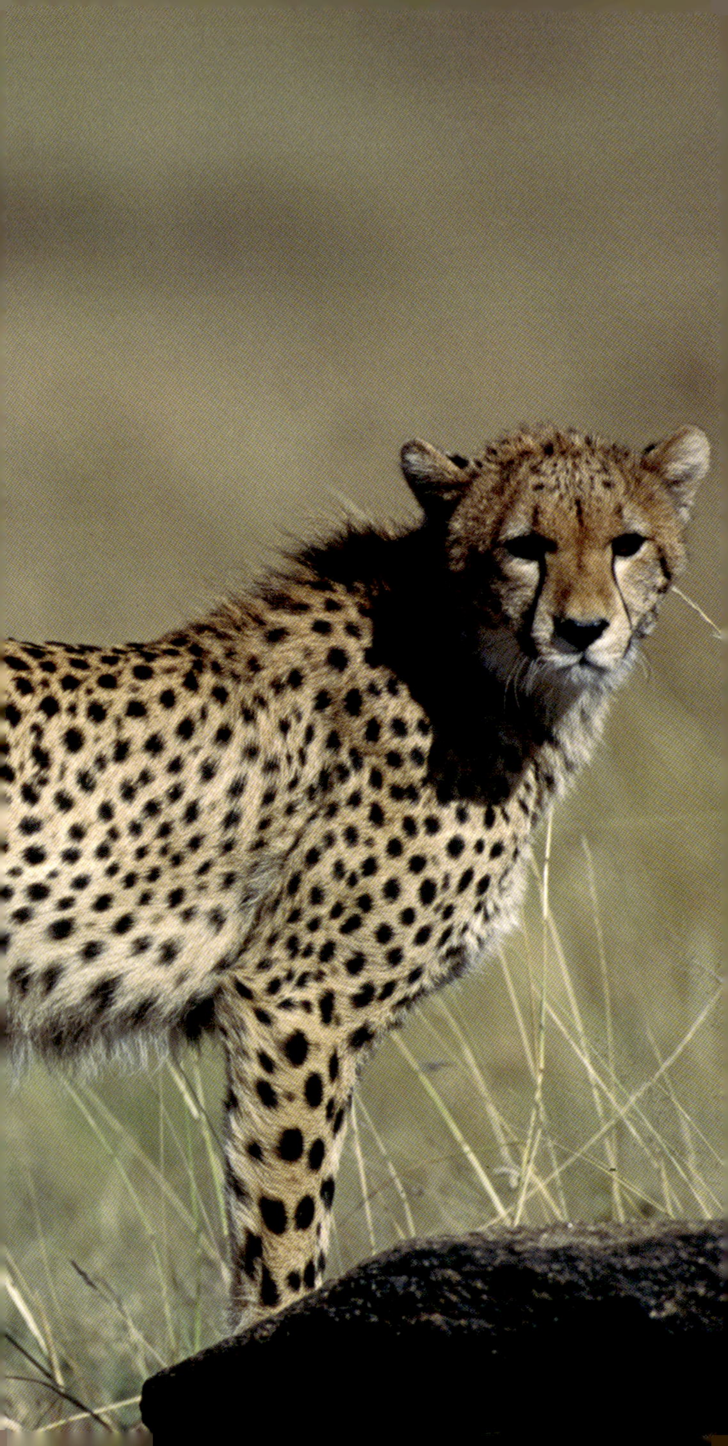

Above: Large cheetah family wait patiently for prey to pass in the long grass of the Mara savannah. Cheetahs are the fastest land animals in the world.

Opposite: Young cheetah spies out the land.

A pair of cheetah take advantage of an observation point to look for possible prey.

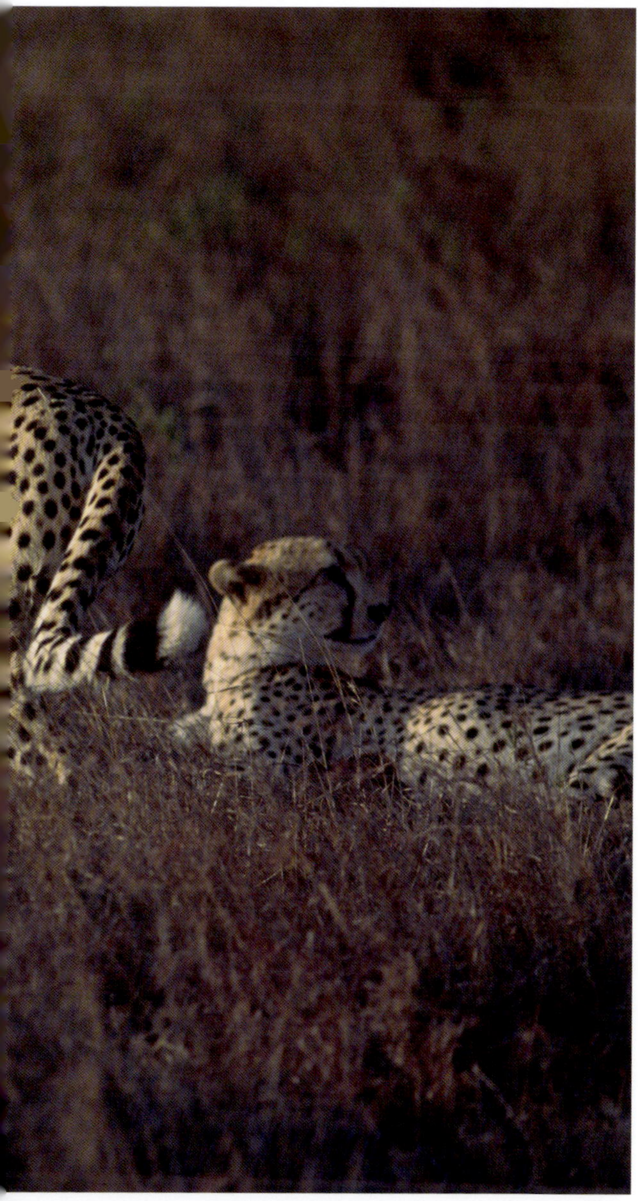

The Hunters – the Big Cats

or so it will give up the chase. Sadly, the cheetah is one of nature's losers. When the hunt is over and the quarry dead, the cheetah lies with heaving flanks for up to half an hour before recovering enough to feed. In that time it is vulnerable and often loses its food to determined hyenas or even jackals. Vultures, too, in great number will snatch the prize literally from its jaws. It is not unknown for a leopard to take advantage of the cheetah's exhaustion and make off with a fresh kill. The cheetah has neither strength nor aggression to resist the robbery.

The cheetah is considered the fastest land mammal and has been timed at 110 kilometres an hour. In the 1930s one of the more eccentric European settlers took a pair of domesticated cheetahs to England, to compete against greyhounds. The cheetahs regularly beat the greyhounds over 400 yards, tricked into persevering with the chase by clever manipulation of the speed of the electric hare.

Cheetahs are mild-natured creatures, rarely attacking an aggressor. When angered they will growl deeply but otherwise utter a curious, bird-like chirruping note, and purr when content. An animal of the open plains, it is usually seen singly or in pairs, unless it is a family party of females with cubs. Infant mortality is high. Two to four cubs are usual, and subject to early predation from snakes, birds of prey, small predators such as jackal and ratel, and the carnivorous members of the mongoose family.

Largely solitary, the cheetah is often observed scent marking its territory. This behaviour is more common among males, and it would appear that the presence of other cheetah within an apparent territory is tolerated. The cheetah has been studied rather less than the lion or leopard, and there are large gaps in our knowledge of the animal's behaviour.

The female teaches her young to hunt by example, and will catch a young Thomson's gazelle – their favourite

The Hunters – the Big Cats

prey in the Mara – and carry it alive to where she has left the cubs, releasing it for them to capture. Cubs and mother are affectionate, playing together and grooming each other. When the family finally does split up, male siblings sometimes stay together for long periods.

The Mara cheetah, perhaps the most beautiful of the cats, can be seen as symbols of survival. While not increasing in numbers at least they hold their own. Against numerous natural odds they survive, and are fairly widespread within the area. Although there has been no reliable count it is estimated there are probably 60 to 80 individuals in the greater Mara ecosystem. Being diurnal hunters they are easily seen, and sadly their hunting attempts, which under natural conditions are frequently frustrated, are further hampered by the ever-present vehicles and tourists. A little more concern for the animal and less for the ultimate kill picture would be welcomed, not only by the unfortunate cheetah but also by the many people who are concerned for the welfare of one of nature's truly magnificent creatures.

An early morning game flight in a hot-air balloon is the high point of a Maasai Mara visit for some.

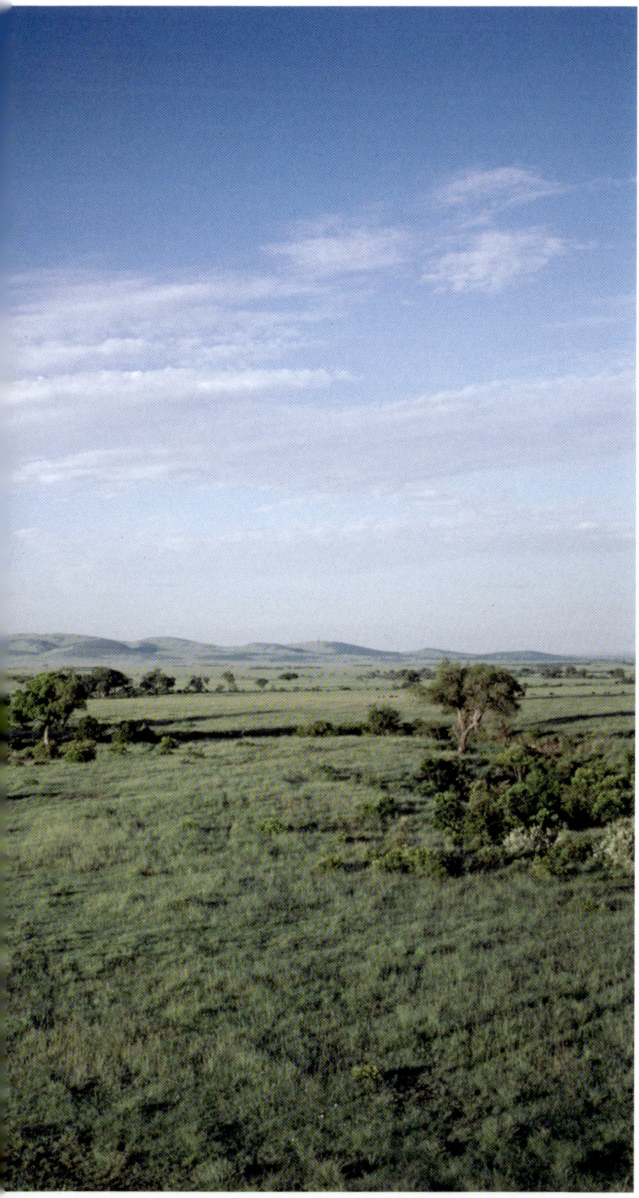

8. The Hunters – the Lesser Breeds

It is seen as a scavenger, a sneak-thief that lives off what it can scrounge, the undertaker for indigenous peoples and an efficient waste disposer. The hyaena is all these, and has few friends – in the eyes of many, a much-maligned animal.

Studies of the spotted hyaena, carried out among others by Hans Kruuk, who worked in Ngorongoro and the Serengeti, prove that they are very much frontline predators, and the most efficient in Africa. Certainly they scavenge, but more effectively than lion or leopard. Their exceptionally powerful jaws can crush all but the bones of elephant, buffalo, rhino and giraffe. As disposers of waste they have no equal.

These proficient killers prey on anything from insects, birds and fish to the young of rhino, elephant and buffalo. They hunt and run down impala and gazelle. At night the cautious, rather furtive character becomes a bold and swashbuckling adventurer. He may decide to raid your camp, chew your boots and old clothing, and upend your cool-box in search of food. The hyaena is detested by the Maasai who have many tales, most of them obscene, of their alleged stupidity and unpleasant habits. Stockmen have made many attempts to get rid of them, often relying on poisoned baits. As a result, hyaena numbers have declined outside game parks and Reserves.

The hyaena's mournful yowling is a common feature of the African night. They have an astonishing variety of grunts, yelps and chuckles, and when excited at a kill or during mating they give vent to a cadence of howls resembling maniacal laughter, hence the 'laughing' hyaena of popular legend. Contrary to popular belief they are not hermaphrodites. The external labial swellings in the female are unusually developed, and may be mistaken for the male scrotum.

Characterised by a massive head hung low, a back sloping sharply to the hindquarters, and an ungainly,

The Hunters – the Lesser Breeds

slouching gait, the spotted hyaena is a familiar figure on the plains. The female is larger than the male, and the species is clan-oriented – each clan with a territory wherein members may have several sets of dens. The related but much rarer aardwolf and striped hyaena, being strictly nocturnal, are seldom seen. Evidence of their presence is more often found as carcasses on the roads, victims of carelessly or murderously driven motor vehicles.

Once considered vermin, to be eliminated at every opportunity, the African wild, or hunting, dog, has acquired almost cult status during the last 20 years. They have been the subject of much research and elaborate coffee-table volumes. Wild dog are thoroughly disliked by the Maasai, who consider them greedy and dangerous and a menace to domestic stock. However, in recognition of the species' social organisation and communal care, they believe that there is always a pack leader, respected by the others. During heavy rain the pack will shield the leader with their bodies – hence the Maasai expression that an excited *moran* should be treated like the pack leader, smothered and restrained.

Wild dog are probably presently locally extinct in the Mara, but are still found to the south, in Serengeti. It is generally believed that disease is largely responsible for reduced numbers. *Rickettsia canis* and rabies are suggested as the most likely causes. There may be some connection with growing human populations and a parallel growth in the numbers of feral dogs. As they run in packs and live closely together in burrows when breeding and raising young, infection will spread quickly.

Wild dogs hunt rodents, hares and the medium-sized-grazers – such as impala and Thomson's gazelle. There are records of wild dog pulling down wildebeest and young rhino. The size of the quarry may be related to the size of the pack – larger packs taking larger animals. When hunting they rely on teamwork. They decide which animal to cut out

Above: A pair of rare black rhinoceros in the Maasai Mara.

Opposite: One of Africa's famous Big Five – Cape Buffalo, notoriously ferocious when hunted or wounded.

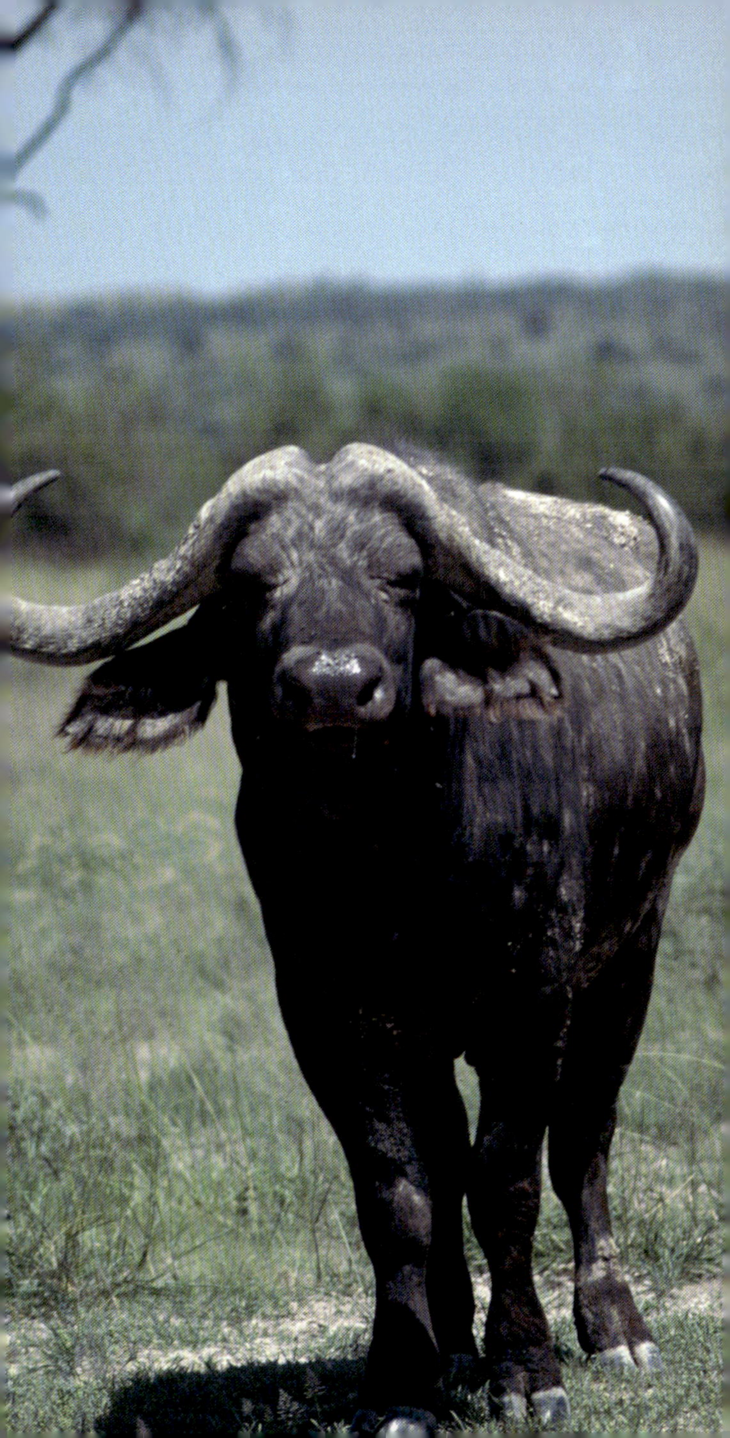

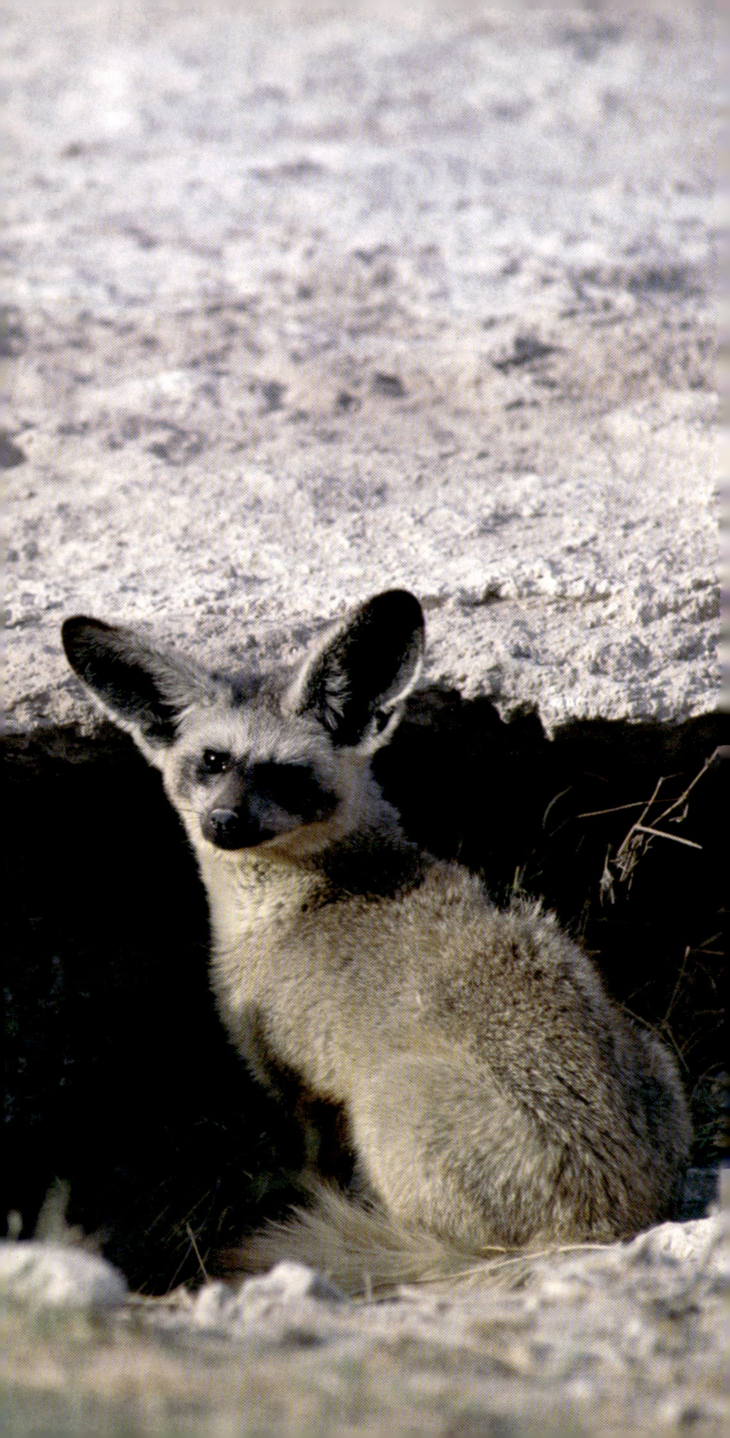

Above: One of nature's smallest predators – the silver-backed jackal, often seen skulking around lion or hyaena kills ready to dart in and steal morsels.

Opposite: Bat-eared fox shelters from the midday sun in the shadow of an overhanging rock.

The Hunters – the Lesser Breeds

of a herd and one or two dogs chase it remorselessly, with the remainder of the pack jogging comfortably in the rear. As the leading dogs tire, so others take up the chase until, as the victim flags, it is pulled down and quickly torn to pieces.

Striking characteristics of the wild dog are the large, upstanding ears with rounded tips, patches of sandy rufous and white markings on a basically black skin, and always a white tip to a fairly bushy tail. They are usually silent, though on the kill they will utter whimpers of excitement and curious chatterings. A call is given by a short bell-like tone with lowered head and with frequent pauses for listening. The call often results in a reunion with other pack members. The young are fed regurgitated food by both male and female adults, and litters may be as large as 16 whelps.

Of the smaller carnivores the three varieties of jackal are frequently seen, the most common in the Mara being the silver or black-backed. Distinguished by a distinct black saddle, tinged with grey hairs, and pointed and upright ears, they are usually seen in pairs or in unrelated groups on the fringes of lion kills. The much more rare side-striped jackal is more solitary and nocturnal, while the golden or common jackal is seldom seen within the boundaries of the game reserve, but is more likely to be met on the open plains between Narok and the main gates.

The solitary serval is a large wild cat with a white band on rather large oval ears, and a rufous, tawny and spotted coat. It is a handsome animal, seen in grassland on the plains when stalking snakes or small rodents. One of the most courageous animals of Africa, the ratel or honey badger, is seldom seen though not rare. It is partial to honey and grubs found in beehives. The honey-guide, a small bird fond of the wax in honeycombs, will often lead the ratel to hives in hollows in the ground or at the base of trees. The ratel's tough skin makes it impervious to bee stings and, while it feeds on the grubs and honey, the honey-guide contents

The Hunters – the Lesser Breeds

itself with the wax uncovered by the ratel's digging – a perfect example of cooperation in the wild.

The attractive little bat-eared fox is regarded as harmless and fun by the Maasai – and so it should be. They do not occur in large numbers, but can be seen in family parties in the early morning and evening. They are principally insectivorous, but also eat small rodents and the nestlings of ground-nesting birds. Their enormous ears, black faces and legs with a typical fox-like brush make this small creature a delightful subject to watch.

In similar localities, troops of banded mongoose, a sociable diurnal species will certainly be seen, sooner or later, on any journey within the Maasai Mara. When crossing the open plain in a rope-like chain, some will stop to balance on hind legs and stare curiously at whatever might be disturbing them, before careering onwards to disappear headlong down the tunnels of a termite hill, from which anxious heads will be seen poking up in curiosity. The last two species are part of a large group of small carnivores, consisting of five species of mongoose, the civet, Zorilla and wild cat and, in the rivers, the clawless otter, many of which may rarely be seen, but which are an integral part of the Mara mix.

Pack of hyaena lie in wait in the Maasai Mara. Long regarded as scavengers, hyaena are also perhaps Africa's most efficient hunters.

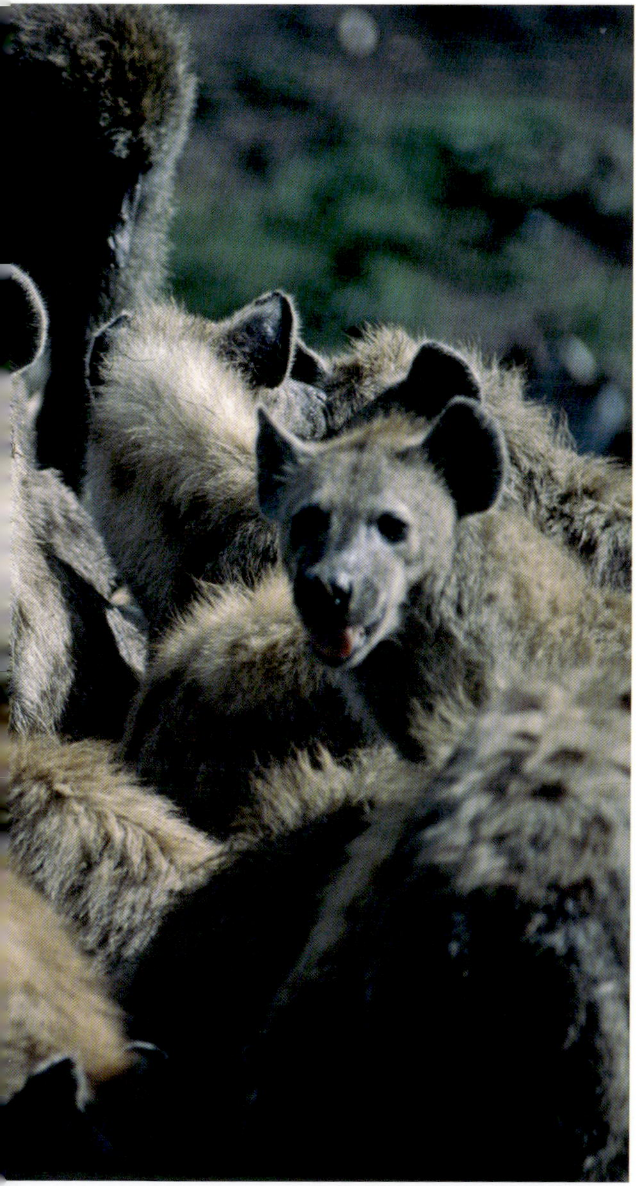

9. Those who also have their being

The ubiquitous warthog is commonly associated with the Mara plains. Conspicuous wart-like lumps protrude on either side of the face; the upper tushes are large, curving upwards, and used mainly for digging. Normally seen in pairs or family parties, warthogs are entertaining characters to watch. When startled they run with tails erect and if pursued by a predator, can reach a spanking pace, side-stepping and swerving as elusively as a star footballer. They feed kneeling on their front legs and adopt the same attitude when drinking. Leopard and lion are their major enemies. Warthogs are spirited and truculent opponents when under attack – an old report from the Uganda Game Department records that a fight between a lion and a warthog resulted in the death of both. The two animals were found dead a few metres apart. The lion, a full-grown young male, had a deep tush wound which had penetrated his ribs and, presumably, his heart and lungs. The warthog was badly mauled. Warthogs normally lie up in old burrows, which they enter backwards, ready for rapid flight if danger threatens.

The male ostrich, more than two metres tall and capable of three-and-a-half metre strides to reach a speed of 50 kilometres an hour, sports bright pink thighs when breeding. The black-plumed males and drab hens conduct an elaborate courting ritual. The male sits on its long legs rhythmically beating its wings on either side, rubbing his neck along his back. The hens are often unimpressed by this odd behaviour, but may decide to respond with an alternate ruffling of their own wings, combined with a series of darting runs. The ancient Egyptians regarded the ostrich as a symbol of justice, having noticed its feathers have vanes of exactly equal width on either side of that shaft – unusual in a bird. Most species have feathers that have one wide and one narrow vane, and so are unjustly divided. The Egyptians were the first to use ostrich feathers for adornment and, of

Those who also have their being

course, centuries later the plumes became important fashion accessories in Europe and America. In many parts of Africa, ostrich were farmed commercially to supply the market, and today there is a revival of the business, certainly in Kenya. Some Nairobi restaurant menus offer the meat, which is fatless and nutritious. The skin makes durable leather for handbags and wallets.

The cock ostrich assumes much of the parental care after the hen has laid the eggs, incubating at night, while the female incubates during the day. They are principally plant eaters, but also eat large grasshoppers and lizards.

Another distinctive bird is the long-legged secretary bird. Its name is derived from the long, black-tipped plumes that protrude from the back of the head, as did the quill pens of clerks in counting houses and offices in the old days. Predominantly black and grey, the bird stalks across open country with high stepping strides as it looks for snakes, grasshoppers and small rodents. They are capable of delivering a powerful downward blow with their legs and often kill quite large snakes. They build large, untidy nests in flat-topped trees, normally laying two eggs.

No traveller through the Mara will fail to notice the vultures, of which six species occur, seen soaring on the thermals or crowding round a predator's kill or the remains of a natural death. It is common to find no less than five species congregated when feeding – the white-backed, white-headed, hooded, Ruppell's and the Nubian or lappet-faced – the biggest by far. The likely absentee will be the Egyptian Vulture, mainly white, which favours drier areas.

The marabou stork, is a familiar figure close to lodges and camps and near rubbish tips. The adults develop a large air-filled pink pouch that hangs from the front of the neck, the function of which is obscure. The marabous join the vultures and eagles in soaring with the rising thermals, their sharp eyes alert for signs of carcasses or prey.

Warthog in the Maasai Mara.

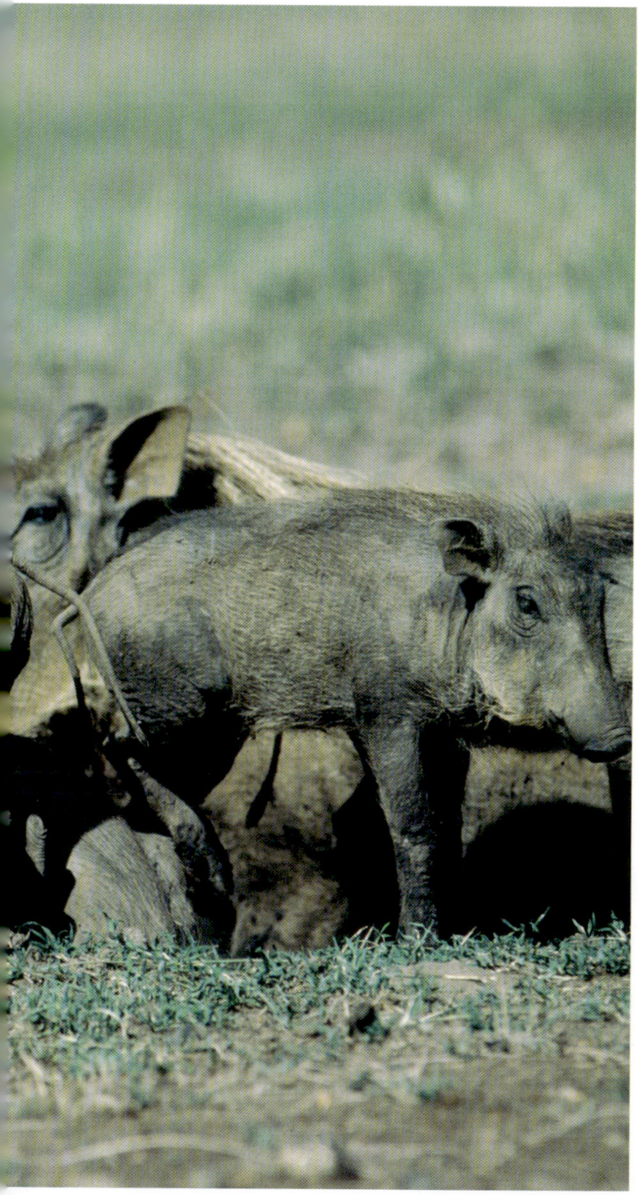

Those who also have their being

The short-tailed bateleur eagle is one of nature's most accomplished soaring birds. It glides for long periods with no apparent movement of its outstretched wings, until it wheels and plummets earthwards to rise with a snake held firmly in its talons. The impressive martial eagle, the largest in Africa, will stoop from a great height to pick up a small Tommy or impala, though its usual food is guinea fowl, francolin or hyrax.

While the large birds capture the eye through sheer size, the plains are alive with brightly-coloured movement, even in the shimmering haze of midday. The male yellow-mantled widow bird, the scarlet shoulders of the red bishop, the rosy-breasted and yellow-throated longclaws, the speckled quail, the rich lilac throat and breast of the lilac-breasted roller, and the crimson wings of a turaco at the edge of forest or bush streak vivid splashes of colour amid the greens and browns of the plains.

The most common of the monkeys are the baboons, seen everywhere. Together with the lively vervet, or black-faced guenon, they are unwelcome visitors to lodges and campsites. Both are inveterate thieves and, being accustomed to humans, commit outrageous thefts of food and belongings from unwary visitors. Other species are the blue, white-nosed, patas and Colobus monkeys. They are less visible, and the Colobus is found only in forested areas. Bushbabies, the greater and lesser galagos, are more likely to be heard than seen. The loud squalling cry, like a bad-tempered baby, will be heard after dark among trees, where they are most at home.

Crocodiles are found on the banks of the Mara River. They are supremely efficient cold-blooded creatures, able to keep themselves close to a constant heat – in the water, out in the morning sun, back in the water again when it gets too hot, out in the evening and in the water again when the sun is too low to warm. Lethal to small, unwary animals that

Those who also have their being

come to the water's edge to drink, crocodiles profit from the wildebeest migration, feeding on those that perish at the river crossings.

Snakes are not popular, and few people would go out of their way to look for one. They have their devotees, however, and they play their role in nature's scheme by feeding on rodents, which, if uncontrolled, reach undesirable numbers. The largest snake is the python, which may reach six metres in length. They favour river banks and rocky outcrops and with their large jaws and recurved teeth are capable of inflicting nasty wounds on a victim. Happily, they are shy and would rather slip away quietly than make an unprovoked attack. They are unique among snakes in having sensory pits on their lips, which enable them to locate warm-blooded prey in the dark.

In the end, the most enduring Mara memory is the image of the savannah country and open plains, and those creatures that dwell there. Some are rarely seen, others oblige the camera with unfailing regularity and courtesy. It is those animals and sights that give the Mara her splendid image, and no journey through the magnificent grasslands and bush is complete without them.

Impala

Herd of elephants roams through the luscious Mara grasslands.

125

10. Images

The Maasai Mara is a treasure house of wildlife, large and small, colourful and drab, spectacular and insignificant. For so long as it fulfils its role in Kenya's vital tourist industry it will attract controversy and command attention from planners, advisers and conservationists. But controversy and the Maasai Mara have been partners for many years. No one can predict the future, or foresee what nature may have in store. Disease may decimate the wildebeest herds; fire, flood or famine may impose irresistible pressures on the land and its wildlife.

The Mara is but a small part of a greater ecosystem – the Serengeti – and its future fortunes are irrevocably bound to what happens in that vast and important area. Things will change, and it would be unrealistic to think otherwise. There will be a greater emphasis on fencing and enclosure of land. There will be further limitation of range and degradation of habitat. The Mara, however, has shown great resilience and withstood many pressures in the four decades since the National Reserve was created. The people of Kenya are more aware than ever that wildlife is part of the beauty and wealth of their country and worthy to be preserved. The parks are no longer looked upon simply as playgrounds for the rich and foreign. There can be no room for pessimism and apathy. The story of the Maasai Mara is far from over, with many chapters yet to be written. Confidence must reign that the beauty of the Maasai Mara will endure, to be enjoyed and rediscovered by future generations.

> Let John Milton have the last word:
> *Accuse not Nature, she hath done her part;*
> *Do thou but thine.*

Above: Ostrich hen and brood stroll the Mara plains.

A cheetah gazes out over the plains of the Mara.